…TRACKING… THE MASKED DAWN

POEMS

Brian Brogan

TRACKING THE MASKED DAWN

Brian Brogan

Published by Dog Heart Land Press
https://dogheartland.com/dog-heart-land-press/

Edited by Kevin Del Principe
Cover art by Brian Brogan

ISBN 979-8-9867804-0-5 (paperback)
ISBN 979-8-9867804-1-2 (e-book)

10 9 8 7 6 5 4 3 2 1

Dedicated to Jessie and Sean

Also by Brian Brogan, The Hailing Light of Bees

CONTENTS

TRACKING THE MASKED DAWN

For this journey I paint my body with beeswax
brushed deep golden hues of peyote lizards
swimming through crystalline tunnels of light

Their reptilian split tongues and ultraviolet scales
animate a translucent radiance, a flow of mirrors
under the emerald sea pursuing
the holy singers of dawn

They envisage my water-drumbeat
as a gray boat of bloated cities on the offing horizon
beating escape from the dark underbelly of civilization
perceptions bulkhead scraping
yearning voices and ambrosial desires
for the queen's cell in underworld compression
I walk spellbound through the hex-agons
and glistening mescal buttons
in the winter seabed of my ribcage

My pathway trails kelp and starfish
curative whale soundings
cocoons of moonlight
inside wounded and dead bodies
echoes locating clefs of pensive grace
perfumed with images of little mercies

I am joined by a colossus mythmaker
crusted in barnacles and brine
she makes stride with powers of the wave
remote-sensing her way to the north star
hauls my driftwood keel and Big Dipper
for star map-making into the mouth
of a volcanic archipelago
she pours her Qi's vital power

glassy glimmering aphanites beckon
from each grain of black magnetic sand
attracting Luna moths to light
to guide the transparent dreamtime

Don't let the darkness turn back inside you
playing dead to the exploitation of the sacred
all things inside your submarine pinging heart
Dive among the repository of moats and dead star
ashes of ancestral cratered dreams
in the dark interior of your journey
invite your spirit creatures and ghosts
trapped between worlds
into alliance and alchemy

Your soul and theirs
travel the spindle neurons
behind my whale mask
Whale of other worlds reflected
in your nubilous depths
all your thoughts about death, imps of darkness
harpoon, gillnet decompression, purse seine

The neocortex watches the predatory squid glow
concealed in a disguise of counter illumination
tentacles entreating barbed logic traps
desensitized self-serving rationale

With a lightning trident I draw the needed curative
on the burnt skin of a sunken war canoe
its old hull fills with fantastical animals
Marine iguanas painted in ochre, blue deer precepts
feathered weavings of invisible turquoise bird
offerings hung from the serpent pillars
of my inner temple

I grip the centerline yoke and throw

our petrified rope of empathic lights
over the gunwale, follow me if you choose
I know not where
Somewhere in my lizard-headed dream
To whatever darkness we must go through
To track the masked dawn
through cracked human edifices

Undertows ameliorated by unbearable
patience carry what you have sown
for others, bear your overflowing testimony
to the death scales of our planet
your grief and hopes about the great beyond
Your unfolding hermetic keys
of psychopompic funerary art
cowritten lyric composed in the breath
of the Creator's song
life and death syzygy
vibrating through all forms

Bring your desert self that once was ocean
Your limestone mushroom, swan reed,
red berry fungi, your porous aquifer
your bone mineral reflections
of primordial travels
circling the great shroud
of cyclic lunisolar memory
fading and returning shore waves
rolling skies, oblong orbits, scything crests

You paddle, I'll guide the blood moon tide
in rhythmic call and response
Bone whistling into the seismic
spirit traveler's highway

Listen to the hive-headed deer telling our story
to the solar queen bee's egg's

Ironwood coyote materializing prophetic poetry
as a visionary sacrament for the lost world
inside the spineless cacti

Colonized roots of our living word, honey fueled
breath through cloudburst and titanic birds
carrying astrological charts in prehistoric flowers

Future log entry:
I see the moon spread across braided pearl waters
Songs of bees and crow tribes
coursing east over the bone middens
and sky flower whorls

Outlier spirits drift above the lake valley mud
cracking solar eggs into the maw
of a voracious fog bank

I see as an elder-child
the lizard angels, Gila monsters whispering
inside the red dwelling places of extraterrestrials

Worlds within worlds
in the tide pools of empty faces
The end time of humankind brimming
with futile gravestones and birthstones
in the crushed diamond sutra

Myriad masquerades of egotistical blind power
glitter behind the death mask
Sleepwalkers roam aimless
above slag heaps of mute embers
mumble star-throated ghost words
severed from source
Undreamt vision perishes
disembodied from the earth's mantle
they are floating red-veined leaf hearts

drying-out in vaporizing illusions
I chant Ghost Ghost Ghost
But there's no ghost dance left
Everything's changed and ghosts don't dance
through the gray films of reality
The coyote has little to watch less to track
Disappears into the dried leaves
whispering not me not me

I put her desert spirit balm into my spine ladder
Rattle a wooden egg of unknown dormant seeds
into arcing waves of animal consciousness
I run, rubbing creation fire into the pads of my feet
Moon burns red across my chest Yip Yip Yip
My jackknifed wrist moves
through the acculturation shackle
into an ancient square spiral
Delivers new moons pirouetting
on the pine needle dance floor
I chant trickster trickster TRICKSTER
unravel the old sands of time
in the riddled thunderheads

My rain cloud tattoo rolls past
with my hand shaking
interplanetary lifelines
in the cinereous stillness
I chant rain rain RAIN
flood earth halo lights into the lacuna
volley a Yin Yang reel for the ghost dolls
cooling and splitting, releasing
all that's left after forty billion years
into oracular stories, revived earth languages
Animal clicking sounds rise from the sward
Eclipsed protean moons ooze
up from the heaving permafrost

Don't worry that's my leg charging
with Caribou spirit
through the chthonic barrens
squashing red berry into supernova
Take a breath all is not what it seems
this will soon be over

Cactus goes back to stiff-ribbed needle spines
snagging the passage of horsehairs whinnying
calligraphic soft eloquence into the wind
Stalking puma goes brazenly home to talk with cave
ahead of the fangs, deer is not lost
The sun barks out of the deer's mouth
a grotto for daemons will be our land now
Words are closer to the world soul now
Now, now where I have always been
obsidian's reflection of light
from the waning crescent's last hour

If you don't understand
the language of wild dance
I chant stone stone STONE
Shout through the marrow gateway
the dance of a stone has a long way to go
sliding cities into the ocean
cracking continents in the howling deep

I'm talking to the black
painted face of undying death
who says there are ways
to make the earth grow inside us
to call it home, but only if we practice
long in the spirit tongue
Stomp our feet
to the shaman's mystery babble
drum cracking STONE
in the marmoris pelvic bone

to make yellow flowers grow up
from the petrified horizon
A great luminescent egg rises
and hovers in the air between us
eases my burden
of carrying the sacred
into matter

I travel with white crystal quartz babies
breathing heavy in a spiral tube
From briny shore to terra firma core
each of our Earth creatures
roam inside our bodies
looking through our thoughts
Such thoughts are not always mine alone
Sometimes I am dusk inside a tree
with eyes turned inward
Sometimes my black-inked limbs
move on their own
tossing about like a drunk mystic
swaying inside the sea's dream

Not far off I see myself returning
from behind the underworld mask
with life in the balance inside my changing form
There's a sunflower with a face in each seed
See for yourself your feelings are recorded
in plants and trees, in the gray gnarled husk of shell
concealing inner abalone color
in the crop circle vegetation glyphs
helping bees with amatory dreams
find tomorrow's effloresced field

This story is truer than most
Shaped like an egg inside a geodic cavern
Oath-bound to a council of sacred precepts
Written with birthing pain

with charcoal and reed
All glazed and preserved
in caches of silence
invisibility and emptiness
Encased in a volcanic-glass holy bead
wedged in the tectonic stress
of an impact crater's fault line

Our broken covenant unravels humanity
Vainly barking not me NOT ME
It may be that you're in here with me
Some flickering light in the ice cave
straining to hear through the dust of light years
some premonition in the horse latitudes
Music of our blue sphere staggering
looking to sing again from astral memory
Look inside the weave of her harvest basket
Everything is closer than you think
Beyond what you've dreamed

GLASS OF A MELTED STAR

Swimming backward
in the sun whorl of a living fossil
I unlearn everything
Waves of perception and sentience
drift in dissolving ions
Bioluminescent droplets hang
suspended in this tubular nautilus
protean stars in the deep

I spume prismatic hues of pelagic origins
up the split stone face of the world
Spiraling white spray in thermal lift
buffets trembling leaf of fern
In the scouring rush
from under scree
I hear the winds of myself
in the solitary mare's tail
The clicking divination sound
in the hare's ear
whose clear fine-spun beauty
pierces the

bleached fox jawbone
deep in my chest
bite of consciousness yips
Is the ragged sea without water

How will I remember my animal
body's heightened senses
The auroras of the wild-word impulses
through the synaptic fruit of my thoughts
Just the one-word kernel
in the chemical crystal lattice
between Alpha and Omega

that can throw love of tree light
spark of stone, into the dead, to reignite

Its sole mellifluous sound
kindles rose of dawn photons
into humus - grows pomegranate heart
through skeletal stone
Swims the prehistoric valley of the whales
through wavelengths of floating countries
Square black clouds with no center of gravity
tethered to thin sheaves of glass words
refracting our solar blind spots
turning us over in our skinny nest
evaporating memory and meaning
dragging easy prey into camouflaged dens

Tossing inside my dreaming grist
devolution radiates through my soluble walls
hinterlands of the soul, cacophony of creatures
I am summoned from this aquatic membrane
I slap my fin and Indra excites red sprites to dance
inside my neocortex stimulating Deep Space
The air glows in my lower dantian manifold
I shoot green spores
through wormhole into mesosphere
into the terrarium of now now NOW

Here where all realities convene
before and ahead of my time
to end and embark again in the expanding galaxy
Double glazed as lightning in parallel worlds
a bolt from the anvil flashes and ashes
I am forged transparent and undivided
My extinct courting swan paddles towards me
Returns through the glass of a melted star

TO SEE WHERE I AM

To see where I am
I sketch to see where I am not
And to see where I am bound
I shrink myself down or expand
in color, words or sound

Before things break up my image
or replace my tone with shadowed droning
I am already gone
ahead of the dead world closing in

But I do not know all of me
in silence and resonance
Is it the wind that is my beingness
Or am I the atmosphere everywhere
In reflections that appear and vanish
am I the bear and wolf I painted
who return to stand in my eyes
just before sleep
Or the giant shade figure
standing by the door waiting for me
Are these my thoughts returning
from three thousand years ago
through beauty relearned
Massive shaman that rises behind me is it me
Odin's voice or the stag
piercing my body

Am I the sadness of humanity
or stone slowly swallowed by this earth
sinking deeper to become the tumescent skin
of a great spherical being

Am I my own micro cosmos inside time

Time outside of known time
Time within time, space in-between known space
or the afterthoughts of someone else's dream

Still my fingers keep on being fingers
moving along the skin of thin realities
It seems I am never done with myself

That which has no name is that me
If what comes next is nothing what will I call it

I feel the trees' attention splitting me
drawing my double into a symbiotic relationship
The bear returns inside me
I think the bear could not be me
Bear thinks I am the same bear
Lonely for nature
for things that are not human
Germination, hibernation, ice floes

Sometimes I disappear, and where to
And when I return
pieces of me are still gone
They only partly remember me
They beckon from great distances
Spellbinding bears
incubating my formless consciousness

Sometimes I reanimate as an ancient solar swan
Sometimes as a ruminant in the spontaneity
I am the apple orchard of forty-five years ago
Sometimes sweet sometimes rotting
surrounded by salt marshes
the musk of hay and animals
crows diving through the coastal air
the sea aching in my heart
Who called me to be here

Who knows me in these appearances
How might I sound to the deities
when many of my words are ghosts seeking form
they might freeze in the air or melt in the spring
They might turn inward or outward like rain drops
expanding or shrinking clarity
How are we forged together with the deities
The blueprint of you and I in each other's lives
our design surveyed and appraised

If I stop questioning these things what will happen
If I don't who or what will answer
will I know when I become someone
or something else
The silent answer is many layered
vibrating membranes
visionary fragments of the future and other worlds
At the base of the skull is where the mind probes
the portals to the origins of space and time
worming through ancestral and primordial memory
to find the communal opening
in the heart's meaning of love
This is the way into the unifying
principle of the universe
to all kind words that will be ever used

My Earth body is made of Earth words
that have bodies of their own
They emerge out of the earth
and return to earth as water vapor and animals
cones of evergreen that fertilize fecund earth anew
My words as I see them now
are a mask of flowers revealed
They are hives kept in a ceremonial healing blanket
Harbingers humming the medicine
of foresight for severed dreams
They are thunderbird shields

Fertile lightning's illuminating flash of who I am
passing across the savanna and under the sea
Inside the blue fir, talking to you and me

BRIEF SHADOW SONG

Unplug yourself from the ghost of life
all the entries that describe you
as the last person down the hall
no one understands
A stranger that travels beneath
the leather sun
All meaning extracted
from the corralled herd
you have become sea glass
worn polished but no longer clear
Search for triggers that blaze the soul
with tender exaltation of wordless knowing
the tears run away that almost blind you
bind you in love

Keep searching for the lucid passage
try reading the slow curve of the day
Swirling wolf hairs in the eddies
scribing the earth for you
in river to sea words
release your see lanes
Driftwood guitars find their way
breathe beneath the sea
Parts of you you thought were gone
fell out of this world
to reunite in this other you become
something you cannot teach touch express
The song words of giants inside your body sheath
keep sharpening the horizon
vacuuming the dust from eyelids
stretching your presence beyond
the piercing bone whistle of your skeletal cage

Sound of planets in the scales of vertebra

following soul tracks
through Earth's deep immensity
Everything stirs and moves in me
to the planets beginning before blue
before seed and green before green
a story pulled from the sky to rest on
to heal gray hues of shadows worn

Behind her mask of mud and straw
the owl hole of shivering silver branches
wings spread through my hands
brush my thoughts, rearrange my life
over rain-pocked ice through saplings
over logs and bark flakes in the deep
wintering of my life
the owl foot in my next step
yellow skin and talons lifting off ice crystals
into the long moon
Silent owls of my body language
giving the wind a ride
emptying the complexity of many selves
into murmuration place, where later in life
we can see teeming omneity in contour

Ephemeral wings flying medicine
beats into skirmishes with the self
moving through the disparities of polarity
tethered birds released from the marionettes
storming thought
our clouded nature
dissolving into itself

I have died here many times before
seeking beauty in the calm wilds
of hive consciousness
In the fevered fauna night
I drink the inner bark of pau d'arco

dreaming my spirit roots through the earth
I hold the drum's inner village up
for the wind to play the life cycle song

My body hears the whale heart
in the verdant water beads, flowers grow
though the small energetic heart of snake
moth wing in the court of clouds
gripped by a presence
winged beings flutter at my cradleboard
beat and chant their memory into mine
Many will recognize me as one of their own
For others I'm a poem that drifts out of reach
Only a few will see and feel roses beneath snow
Paint or carve me in their art
Inside cave walls they stand next to me
With ancestral medicine they open me up
Everything goes through the clan's totem
and returns through me like this ascending
scrawl conjuring worlds into form

WANDERER HARBINGER CARTOGRAPHER

Wanderer harbinger cartographer
I keep forgetting my many names and vows
I burn through the day knowing the night
can devour me with riddles and void
with cracked clouded eyes
stalactite dripping tongue
Journeying in the embryo of the dark goddess
in the memory-rivers woven
to make her forest dress
to make my vision possible
as a brujo wearing silver wolf hair
raven feathers and pine soot markings

The horizons burn I have set sail
This far inland the sea cries in me
I am a starfish inside the whale
blazing in its thin fabric of consciousness
A magpie hand in the ash mound
churning life stories into Chinook winds
A bee hand in the small flowered heart throne

I am inside you when you turn
your thoughts my way
when you sense the other within
ripening the berry of the dormant heart
All things bloom when we pay attention
Sad feint guitar strings remember
long-gone valleys red with your blood
Your tender thinnest branches
have been on the longest journey
through clouds that sharpen the horizon
into blue rivers, silhouetting old mountain bone
saints of death, I am a ravaged glyph returning
A faded handprint still working its way through

Wrinkling maps of time in the before time

When we knew birds sang rain
and muddy ponies put spells on apples
That the ant climbed the reed spire to the sun
gathering the wisdom of the dew
bending blades of grass to hear the earth's decree
That all things live inside the other
That the sheen on evergreens might be enough
to teach us for the rest of our life
That the visit of a spider can rearrange our plans
Rearrange our insides until we have many eyes
Can walk sideways with nimble grace
Can fly with light-filled thread
scattering flocks and pollen into poetic
communion resurrecting presences
on the footpath and in restless dream
slight tears in the beautiful harvest of awareness

This story is too old for most of you
and I'll tell you things you'll soon forget
But return if you are ever kind to my kind
and we will start again

Your sharp arrows were made with feathered endings
Your compass needles were to penetrate
the earth's fading story

The distance between us
is in the dream running heights
It's in the moon with no motion
or sound in her womb
But when the sun leaves
the moon turns on reflection
beats her long drum to return
the distance within
Their tassels of a new dawn

lay over the blue curvature of Earth
Luna and Solar chasing each other in love
Day and night hummingbirds feed
on the sugar of their thoughts
Their musing is disguised
in the many changing faces
of genius loci in the soft turtle sky
and colliding clouds

I hear the dogs barking for the world to be whole
Bullroarers amplifying the sky's syntax
hurling smoke rings and bird shine
through the watchtower of my body
Orphaned words return to ferment the soul
Bells of unconsciousness ring
through statues of space and time
Cities of failed light tolling in dissolution
Bells that can't be heard
in great halls of the crowded mind
Between pages of ornamented history
Kali Yuga who translates your blank page
what we can believe what we can receive

Parables in exile, moss clinging to inert cold
over-hanging the precipice of a river gorge
Emptying out always emptying out, beauty and life
Wisdom would not stay on the page for us
burned in a thousand coveted whispers
little deaths soaring to big death in wingless appetite
Drinkers of rain and lightning in bog dark mornings

Raven tribes of the high desert plateau
lure me back to their feathered lair
To the wind's beginning and origin of bird speech
I see the trellis of my murmuring fingers
seed feeding these masked birds in cobalt air
Birds birds birds fill my cave skull

They fly the azure prayer of the mesa face
Feathered specters in our village song leap ecstatic
Sacred whistles trill lonely mystical prisms

Avian Humanoid of the seventh soul organism
I am, or some strange bestial of a man
with bristly hair and wings
I am offering blue cornmeal
to my ancient child bones
laying on an immortal pillow
strung with bells
The coarse staple wakes growth rings
though the ancestral door
The upturned horseshoe blessing
pours daybreak into unknown parts of me
Bells of the land bend back my black ears
fill my hollows with sustenance
swaying evergreens, land spirits press in
They know the most remote places
can be loved, they bind us back
to everything we ever stepped on
and things we thought we couldn't touch
with our thought merchants combing the
past and future with petition and praise

I scratch my bird skull into the earth
returning petrified mountain shadows
back to the sky in trade winds
From the foothills I am watched
by the ancient maize people
I rattle my shaman stones
into the star shined puddle
clay maps of invisible borderlands
With medicine chant I lure you in
let go, let go into this drowning spell
Fall through this muddy mirror
always open before your knocking

Knocking on you before you open
Everything changes, speechless heart
try explaining yourself to yourself
If it's easy you have work to do
Moving the Milky Way's star consciousness
in the darkness with skilled birdsong
with traces of high myth still half alive
with the soul echo of each little thing

Soft pathways to knots of wood underwater
To the mountain's backbone carried by wings
moods of winter fire among masked cliff dwellers

SCRIBE MERCHANT

I am from the wingless bird people
A migrating shape-shifting scribe merchant
And this is my story

In the beginning when the first stars turned on
the black holes were illuminated
This is why you don't know what you're looking for
when you're trying to find something
You might come across
an ancient reflection of yourself
making you feel young and alive
A new profound voice among overrated
spectacles shouting for attention
But this is a dark trap
Burned nets around boulders
Who is it that you attend to
What is lost in you
is lost to the earth and me

When we birds stand on top of other animals
it is to see what they see
To know what they know in shared wisdom
Without competition for wealth and power
we stand lightly empathic
Not heavy like other insatiable beings
scattered in ruination from delusion
blood and culture lost

I am the double-headed birdman
some call the eagle diviner
My augury interprets the will of the ancestors
and the fates of humankind I don't care
for academic accolades in acronyms
I don't like cities or my picture being taken

while cows are moaning for the moon's company
I might rant wildly of inauspicious things
to throw people off controlled foundations
of their paradigm

Sometimes my role as a harbinger
involves odd activities
It's not a chosen profession
but I do like to help out
When my eyes darken
Odin likes to visit me
Mostly we talk about humans
turning away from nature
and our conjuration of aliens
to startle people
from their unconscious behavior
Odin uses some of my black feathers
for an eye patch
for which he is always grateful

As far as I can remember
I have always been homeless
Living on the edge of villages
and carving away walls
between static and primal life, old fires
still burning in the distant mind
Tired emotion you can't live on words alone
Sparingly I pull words from the sky
when I need their nutrients
Some of my words join the soft glow of a comet

I find ways to survive
and my weight is still sufficient
I even have an extra bit of flesh for leaner times
When people knock on my drafty nest hole
I pretend everything is normal
I make the correct facial contortions

Refrain from ruffling my feathers
Because my accent is a dead giveaway
I use a few local words and modify
my skin pigments to make the visitor feel better
You can always count on them
seeing right through me I have lost touch
with mass consensus of normal and it with me
As I have said I am homeless but an outcast too
The lowest common denominator
is talking about the weather but even this
raises the eyebrow too high and tightens the jaw
It's not just my bird beard or foreignness
It's my soul that's unwanted
Because they can't trust their own I suppose
I once brought up how there are only a few
animals left and less trees
I won't waste my words anymore
for their perplexed undertow of anger
If there's nothing I can do to change their thinking
I ask the fox to spook them into restlessness

I am one of the last of my kind
The rest have gone off to fame or obscurity
Either one will damage you
In these fallen times everything I create
has the shortest lifespan
I have three days to make a dent
in the empire's attention span
The mortality rate of each integral artifact
is dangerously low
If they trace me back to my soul source
I am damned
It won't be long before I'm found out
I need to keep mobile and clever
And remain semidetached
from fossilized self-important minds
while being force fed a daily account

of the apocalypse

To keep sane I have put myself into a few
of my poems and there I live
Gargantuan journeys under the mud and flame
A team of archaeologists unearthed
my damaged spirit
Three thousand years from now
they watch my soul rise
while pretending not to notice
over their spades, picks and bulldozers
Over the seven Sitka spruce
plastic turf bags and wind turbines
Over the world leaders, border guards and terrorists
Over the poor and homeless writing
and painting strange things
drawing visits from curious wingless birds like myself
On vacation for a short spell
but around long enough to leave helpful instructions

Although I have learned muse conjuring
from a distant master
and thought the teaching sound
I failed miserably and had to go my own way
And so should you
But if you should pay attention to what I say here
you will resonate with the universal principles
bestowed from your own source

Find a burning sky
that is not perceptibly on fire in your world
Let it penetrate your imagination
with a combustion of heat and light
With your trained eye pick out only
the illuminated letters from the black smoke
Forge their shapes and sounds
into new old words immortally potent

Tender and malleable words
with muscle, heart and soul
Find adjoining words that relate
and make each other feel good
Crown them side by side nobly
respecting each other's entitlements of sovereignty
Words of a fiery mix, creating hybrids
of your DNA that draw from other worlds
Words that won't wash away or cool off
with distilling voices of the critic and novice
Words as trusted bridges between flesh and soul
without wounds to drown occasionally
They must canter sensually for the listener
but overall they must arc like predators
and sink like raucous death
They must not smell after being in a cave
for three years that's the test
They must be able to abide in solitude
and deep silence indefinitely
They must be able to ripen
and grow an olive orchard in ancient Greece

Words will be stolen in the current era count on it
But still you must apprentice for their freedom
while holding them together
You will have to keep re-using words
in different ways for the right burnish
But let no one know how you sweated
for the luster to light your way
Keep your poems secret
until the vampires recede at dawn
Don't bother asking Y the B's fly and the I's run
You have no control they have a life of their own
When you die again and again
whole poems will come by and pay you respects
Even the ones you thought no good
and crumpled up disrespectfully

Luckily there's no sin
or punishment in their religion
Some of your favorites might decide to stay
and migrate with you
Choose carefully what these poems say
In your next life you'll be living inside them

Some words have tried
to escape my right turn
only to fall into prose

Keep your words clear and quickened
through inner rites of passage

Let them out to scream once in a while
for being so suppressed as a word servant
Accept the chisel and axe of pop culture
Lonely letters and crowded words
decimated unfurled repeat

Some words might turn on you
while others give epiphanies and euphonies
while sharing coffee
A lone poet is a primeval being
inside an overly domesticated home
Keep to yourself and let it rip
when the owners are away
If they ever invite you back, act confused
but not so much that they have you hospitalized
U and I are calling me now leading me astray
but there's something I need to get across
Have you ever had the experience of a poem
getting inside you and changing you
So watch what poems you create and read
It took me thirteen hours one day
to find myself again

I came back perched on top of a Sitka spruce
with skin bags full of medicinal herbs and spices
A note was pierced and resting on my talon
It read wingless crow merchant
with the deerless queen's blessings
Grant passage across borderlands upon request
He must return to the aviary by noon
or be escorted under civil arrest
All are forewarned and obliged by decree

THEATER OF THE PAINTED STORY

1.

I have been before words
facing one another
Seen their meanings
caught in the middle
without beginning or end

Been between words
hoping life would fill the blank page
Hoping they would go away
or fall out of order

In service to their constellated frontier
In their house of mind tissue
In windows hoping to break free
of reflection

I attached wyrd words in fierce making
Now retreat in words as simple souls
and set them free inside me

A book of wind
Poems of empty space
It takes a whole tribe to feel them
to fulfill who they are

2.

I leave them behind as poem shells
sculptured from ocean chant
I pick them up again
at the shore's edge
You can hear the vibration

in the ear of this one
writhing in the star net

Flame of beeswax heart melting
cold fictions in nomadic memory

Haiku mind carried on the long thin ear of the sea
All words inside me sing their lifelines
into the vast moving mystery
Leave for the unknown shore
where angels with mirror wings
whirl galaxies inside me

3.

Womb of sacred water
I listen hard for verdant plantings
surging gestations
little wings at my door
Purifying rhythm of the old crows
holding the moon in prayer

In the monastery sea light
I do the feather dance wonder
with my eagle head of flame
with my paint blood miracles
for sacred theater in the blue expanse

My space angels know me
by falling out of their world
into this other I become
the stranger's strange story
which is everyone's story
we can't see inside us

You might find these words
when I am dead to this world

I am never truly dead
Uninhabited, expressionless, missing

parts of me go through -

the spring snake
with twig I make
the tongue come out
of the drifting stars
Shed news of our future
Tell us what we need
Bearing the earthly crossroads
into consciousness
flaming on the brink of God
Cicadas write prognostications
together in one song
high-pitched on the sky wall
rain when you ride
their quickened maraca
from hazy cloud
to clear vision
Follow nature's call

4.

Reach, touch, express
acceleration of heart
Maps blaze in the tea belly
Land flow through me
beyond the hedge world
Rip ride the wind
Stretch my presence
to blossom on the fork of birch
with my power bundle of antler and stone
I alter space and object with thought

Invisible white branch on the window

moving a child to a new world
Remnants of an awkward beauty
rustle inside us my friend
Labor of a head grown wing
flies to the nectar of heart

5.

To be more than the hopeful
awaiting goddess
Reverse the upper sentence
for greater wonder than this
I AM awaiting hopeful for her
Yes yes to keep me wanting more

Passage in her floral dress
Dance moves
of fire and fog
Wind in each leaf
One tree at a time
Single address
contained in it all

You
dream you
and learn when you're meant to

A rodeo of zeros
It is everything
It is nothing
Stringed to
many selves
in many worlds
our lessons thunder
thousands of clear visions

I am home far away

where the entrance keeps going
Body veins sparkle
near the vanished state
All edges of life leap
when you are about to be free in life
Passing stars become ships of prophecy

ANIMALIA IN THE LIBRARY OF SOULS

There will be a time
when I won't remember this story so well
Night scatters her ruminations
They collect in puddles
They gather in a spoon by the window
and are swallowed by the witching hour
Hungry dreams, sometimes we can't remember
who we are for good reason
And there are things that take our life
apart for the better
I repeat myself but few have understood
my crumbling perceptions
spread out in the four directions
migrating in the umbra
with Jurassic mineral and pigment
river mind and tree lore
Well below the earth in permafrost sediment
birds both dead and alive
look through my body with lamp black eyes

I was a stone carving
that became a snow-shelled tree
I pulled away from the ice tundra
with feet turned backwards
Drifting through a book of mica schist
I grew hair and snout
Ursa Major swimming against the dark
charcoal currents, distant beginnings
bleeding through worn fences
I'm the bear that wears the bee coat
and a habitable crown of thorns
free from bloody schism

Each bee is a star from the beginning of night flow

swarming with those in the shadow of becoming
strings and rhythms of deeper felt senses
in nomadic windswept memory tents
Elder stories of immense pilgrimages
inside the hive, sacred grove of Animalia
proboscis light pulsing en masse

Under the sleepless moon's holy mesmeric
the skin of birch bark is made from clouds
Holly berry skin of solstice light from the edge of time
Peeper frogs chant doorways open in my body
Each chance is a fast-moving beat
Each choice is a strong beat
Each half sleep is a school - half beat
Each moment of full awareness
a heartbeat beat - hoof beat of pony animus
running for the apple in dawn's stream
Eyes of oceanic constellations
of sad dreams, defused light or reborn stars
Her equus breath is the moon's wind
Ears are the fern tendrils of primeval forest
Her belly is the rustle of nocturnal animals
Underground hooves of basalt escarpment
Mobile statues of time's forgotten history
Coarse hair of war ropes and jaunty
ceremonial games laid down in peace

To know the hearth fire in me
is to know the fire in you and vice versa
Up and down the spine quickening in the pores
the raucous gambling of crows implores us deeper
When you get closer to yourself nothing remains
Old fires some still burning your raw heart
Jeweled strands of creation pushing you to cast off
land on the future, poke stars
in the letters of these words
They are from the wind of Ogham -

trees creaking in the vernal
They are extinct animals
and they are things of power
behind the galactic curtain of fire
Still with us when we're gone

COYOTE POEM

We original coyotes are not the demi-animals
you see today, loping through the disappearing ink
hunting your dream, howling at your lunar thoughts
passing in and out of transient nocturnal cloud

Sitting still in the desert waiting
for your fears to pass in little makeshift fires
as morning star giants shred your shadows
for the serpents to sip through your marrow

We hide behind your ego's rattling dried leaves
We watch the ancient honey drip
for ten thousand years
into your forgotten ash drum
every drop in your subterranean death song
stirring the filters of your aural memory

Crouched inside your prisoner ribcage
we help you tell the wrong story at the wrong time
Slipping into your mind's primordial light
so you'll tell the truth, ripping appearances up
from their tangled roots and concealed caves
Dead parts wasting space inside a guise
the cloistered mirage of consciousness

We make inversed poems
in mnemonic chiastic verse
from our conversations
with the moon's grave tempo

With storms and riddles
we exorcise your over-domesticated ghost
we force you back inside
the metamorphic chambers of the soul

We craft howls that shine so hard
you're apt to grow a tale for the pack
Last night did you hear them
the mournful dead

We werecoyotes, pirate angels, abduct your emptiness
track your wayward thoughts in descent
through the underworld
Call you into our yipping hungry circle
with our haunting windpipes
with your plentiful hands of nothing
to offer as endearment
No bells, beads or colored cloth
just frozen words from stunted hearts
fog of a people with no sense of home

Still we invite you into our stellar den
of dried mud and sand, winding spirals
and reeling crossroads
drum skins and bone shards
Petroglyphs of lightning
bolt from cool walls
to hear your bewildered testimony
Bipedal, world-eating machines
did you cover your tracks coming here

We growl to heighten your senses
to our scent glands and incisors
we are your animal body, the mischievous
spirit creature you sense within and without
We the valued companions of the creator
oscillate between apparition and creature form
Life and death we sing
by the still flame of the moon
ululating sacred curing ceremonies
We are the constellated thoughts
of your ancestors and your death mother

the many-faced she-dog
Her hunting winds break the knotted pines
billowing the dust of generations
Her raven bears raven crazy news
of insatiable ghost people
eating all the beauty
of delicate life, eviscerated myths
unreadable, bound to a dark shelf
the murder of crows
the parliament of owls dying out

Place your skin pouches filled with sighs
on the desert floor, join us
through the gloaming threshold
our shadows are one in gestalt
Forget your name to be inside the mud
matted fur of this other
Return to infant memory
dream rolling in sunlit lupine
Berry smeared sniffing
the motionless mountain's
honeyed meadow
with its swollen river tongue
Salmon undulates at the feet
of the big-boned antlered one
Voice of rogue fires
Vowel sounds of tree roots
sped up and recorded
we hear their root words
and see the vibrating silhouettes
of their breath

We don't have to travel to be with you
We are like rivers moving to the ocean
but already there
Think the distance of coyote thoughts
and interchangeable boundaries will blur

and cohere in sacred imagery
When you forget us we scatter into folktales
When you remember we return
in the mother tongue of all languages
all the verities of existence
passing over what no longer serves the earth

Your ritual call and response brings us home
between the sacred word doors
Transmigration of ancient foundations
pendulum into your restless mind
Speaking in tongues with an unblinking eye
and a crown of fire, you make the vacuum
cleaner break on the hair of the dog
bark-bark bark-bark! woof

We coyotes always size you up
we tear and rend at your comfort margins
with guide ropes and peeling knives
While praying through our fangs
many worlds pass through our alpha root
dispersing seeds into endemic blood memory
Your remembering touch fills
the world with seeds
for the eyes are seeds for insight
the ears are seeds for wisdom
It's with reverent labor you become the seed
The seed dreams of you becoming the seed
Grower, sow what you seek
what we do not know

Earth seeds in the heart hollows
scratching their limestone floors
grow from the fissure of this hairy skin
Ravenous seeds moonless
lonely for the lawless law, free of disguise
Increased in rocky gravitational tides

Moving in the space between words
Behind tectonic walls and inside them
Moving in the gray slate or whale rain
Wind spreading into itself
Beholden to the earth council
with your smoky mirror images
and shapeshifting powers on the way to the sea
with your greeting song masked Coyotl

MEMOIR OF A DISAPPEARING MAN

Preamble:
Did you know there are holes in sound
that cave monks follow
where they mystically receive
the vowelled chants of influencing planets

From the enigmatic sutras of the East
I have read the sound of unadorned beauty
in the hole of an elephant trunk
can tell us more than we could ever learn
from seven lifetimes of seeking inner I's

To alleviate your suffering
practice meditation
with ears of a hunting snow leopard
Filter human detritus
with a blanketing heart of snow

Develop a new internal external
interplanetary transrealism
With soothing sonic texture to quicken you
in this immortal amphitheater
I have created a hole circle of fullness
for travel with words

You can float in the coracle of this round world
and always return to yourself in celestial waves
and still have some substantial form
left over for another day

So as not to dematerialize altogether
in the idiocy of civilization, each time I speak
into this atmospheric refraction
I am building worlds rapidly…

If you were to speak
my incantations without mastery
you would turn eternally invisible and soundless
wordless you'd turn into silence
the presence of pre-manifestation
and presence of post manifestation

A begetting seed without form
for any new or ancient manifestation
Emptiness is an invisible vessel
without walls or facades
Without surfaces of impediment
its nebulous chasm is an incessant
breach of our mind's fortification

If you want to escape
from what I'm talking about here
be a bird that wears an invisible hood
But remember how full circles work
inside my spells and taboos, bear with my dissonant,
enjambment, inconsistencies
while trying to get inside your mind
I'll tolerate your insubordinate distractions

Note to myself:
Be more fluid
Only rain makes me go deeper inside than planned
The Department of Cloudy Interior
states the reason for our feeling low pressure
is the millions of pounds of rain clouds overhead
In the dry lull, I am a tacit silhouette
seemingly careless

Only the sun makes me step out of my body
way ahead of myself
tracking my disappearance at dawn
Only the fruit still on the tree

makes me feel like summer
Suddenly the great distance disappears
in your floating touch
The otherworld permeates my feelings
with serpents and a burning bush
Only the happy and serious dogs
who pleasantly greet me
make me walk off with a purposeful gait
nowhere in particular
I wouldn't mind the insects
making plans without me
But there's never enough Time said Time
And no one would retort
not even Fate or Destiny

Back to you:
We need to discuss current affairs
Research accountants
from the Department of Internal Revenue
have discovered blood cells inside of money
and starting immediately if not sooner
sixty-five-year-olds and younger
will be obligated to donate a mandatory transfusion
Blood money will completely revive our economy
and revise our textbooks on slavery and class
For oh how we wish to stay alive with little minds

Note to self:
Life is turning to brown spots on my hands
While I study the hair trees growing
through these weird little islands
I catch the summer breeze in my next life
Sometimes I wonder what I'm saying
Sometimes I catch up to my wander

Back to you:
War inside is war outside, our mantra, say it

to any festering of self-indulgent turpitudes
The dog barks while you're trying
to pay attention, that's the dog's mantra

Well there are other ways to make poetry
while humanity implodes
I have tried them all in arbitrary moods
or by graceful nature
All these renderings, not my own
but routed through me
hold powerful sway over my weakness
For the dominating muse
I sacrificed my many selves
at the altars of creation
so as not to lose my ground of being
on the eroding Earth (so should you)

But oh how beautiful the accidents
and now - well now
I just can't give my secrets away
but think caterpillars
marching to the moon
Disciples of the far reaches

Testimony of a challenged slack jaw I know
But my thoughts are not always on semi-automatic
with the safety on, OK forget it just listen
Listen and I will get serious for the few of you
who need it and want to get somewhere close
to this unguarded and inconspicuous prose
Long live and prosper with my words on loan

Here's something to read to keep yourself sharp
full of distant pain and sweet things a little too close
We will discuss the nature of reality
and the innards of its polarities
and the incessant paradox of how time talks

to itself without answering back
Pre-genesis Act One will conclude
with the pros and cons of tracking existence
by measuring sensation through the illusions
of finite consciousness

Before we get started
there are two pages written
by twenty-four sages on
communing with the otherworld
at the cost of waking up
And how to manage that babble speech
once you do, Chapter Two
covers how to pretend you're real
I don't remember the other chapters by name
but while I'm thinking about it
see if any of your own erroneous word offerings
hold up in the mirror or crack self-importance

If you're wondering about the natural
disorder of this text there's no telling
where these stories come from
Some unheard-of market with no way to get there
But if you roll with it for the worth of its beauty
you'll get an orbiting pleasure of small
wild clunky gods and goddesses
Their hands are patron saints for my hands
making a plan for you to assimilate a pantheon

For each little holy thing is a seed
you can grow from
Each little holy thing is a world unto itself
interdependent with all other holy things
which is mostly everything in nature
And a good portion of humans too
seem to carry one or two seeds
Which is why I bring these

life-engendering things up reader
in a word or a repeated phrase
yearning for the spell-binding
holy emanating presence, uttering our souls' desire
Rise inside to touch every little holy thing
green fire of the earth, so many can't see

Now, for a cautionary guide-word
beneath our crystallized old selves
surreal wood elves with plastic Spock ears
going to Glastonbury workshops
I'm afraid you are forever banned
from any new era the earth will decide to have
The narcissistic splendor is far too contagious
Others may choose to go back to TV
or a Sedona crystal shop
or to their McMansions
with human mounted heads they hunted
on the way to the top of the food chain
while quaffing libations on grand vacations
at tourist locations in hedonistic grandeur
What is meaningful right now is the unfurling
possibility that we might survive
our adolescent pleasure tumble
inside the earth where we keep
digging holes looking for our missing souls

All our ancestors are down there
Hundreds of thousands of years
of flesh and bone a mass migration
of cellular leeching and seeping
into our vegetables, animals, water and fauna
And we are consuming them or using them for fuel
Oh believe me it's all down there
Why do you think it's called the underworld
Shadowy lineages and vindictive projections
Watch where you reach or put your hands

there are a lot of lonely ones still looking for a host
In a way it's the horror of eating ourselves our DNA
But let me comfort you with a happy ending

More of us are into a make-believe
romantic idea of life, security and comfort
and vain pontificating in fear of the unknown
Creating domain names on Instagrams of self-fame
Tumblr-proof anointings, we can pin
our interests in pictures
we identify with for the whole world
to see our Facebook kudos
regurgitation of information and selfies
lest we forget our beauty and existence
With our face interesting and smiling
and important in a book, web, pod, app
Tweet of our blog blurb, TikTok-ing to stardom
while I excuse myself
but I digressed and compromised myself
to manic media too
How else would you be reading this
But before I close I just want to say
in subterranean societies they say
there's a list of ways to be dead

And you can be somebody else
when you eat them in this zombie apocalypse
A close distant cousin for instance -
I know that in near future times of scarcity
sandwiches will start going on pilgrimages
so as not to be eaten
I know I sound absurd
Until you return in your next life
as a genetically modified double decker
with freshly made reprocessed condiments
free of microplastics
(Someone will take a selfie while eating you

diminishing your man-u-fractured
organic Frankenstein nutrients)
No matter if you're not paying close attention
to what I'm saying, what you have read so far
is entering your bloodstream
If nothing else you'll feel different
when I'm done with you
You'll feel the orbit of the planet quicken
as if the magnetic axis were inside you
You'll gravitate to strange harmonic sounds
far from the maddening crowd
And fierce solar flares will vibrate you slightly
Your mind will be stretched thin
by myriad abstract forms and rigid schooling
from all teacher deities murmuring in your ear
And so on and so on your exhaust
will light the sky for forty billion years
You're probably feeling it right now -

You might come back in your next life
more humble and not want to get involved
or take on any responsibility
for what you know for what you've taken in
... in awareness, you'll only be able to share it
with your closest self
Trust no one when you transcend
This brings me to the last chapter about God
For those of you who have been paying attention
here comes the crowning truth most profound
But before I get into it I will plainly say
I find the carbon dating of my thoughts
to be a little out of date and behind the times
Who am I in the earth strata
in the mythic dream sequence
pre-computer era, post selfie apocalypse
Well what I am not is a righteous drunk
storyteller of nostalgia

with sentiment for hollow traditions
with fantasy befitting one's identity
Or a literary agent with grinds to pick out of his teeth
I'm not a tattoo parlor big on symbols without roots
I'm not lost in the subterfuge of pacifying platitudes
packaged sound bite philosophies
and capitalist markets of words rolling over
themselves covering their breach of integrity
leaches at work in unsustainable blood-letting

Natural kinship ties me to the nocturnal animal
foraging under the bright moon far from its den
Words cannot fully comprehend who we are
unless they stem from the tree of life
nuts, bark and all flowering branches
I started hearing the green words
when I started listening to myself
Gathering even quieter things
between each silence
Two ears and one mouth it's always been said
Anyways I started making my life into a prayer
or more like a fetal bundle of silence
listening to the roots of trees
Body bent inside the falling leaves
of a hollow log on fire with knot eyes ablaze
With spirit vision is how I received my God story
I've been trying to tell you about it and I'll get there
Don't forget what I said
about holes and circles earlier
It testifies to this oracular god encounter
disappearing into my own nature
And this could be useful for your own search
Remember too each little holy thing
For instance, I know a secret the coyote knows
and the rest is just endless pages of footnotes
no one pays attention to
Words saying the same thing into abstraction

I'll tell you a few things that work for me though
I sing irreverent and surreal songs
into the over-domesticated banal conventions
I never allow myself flippant antidotes
I dismiss any recurring symptoms
of sadness for this world
until they come back again
You probably wish to be inspired
most people do, well this is how we get to God
after endless convoluted searching
which is not my fault, and like I said
I hope something in here works for you
Personally I never found much use
for regurgitated knowledge
as a way to insight and wisdom
But a living story that takes on a life of its own
is the unfolding mystery inspiriting the quest
God went missing

He disappeared
Last seen in a Jewish hospital in Brooklyn
named after the desert fathers
and a twelve-year-old rebellious girl named Mary
He was birthed there precocious for sure
but no one claimed him
so we're still looking for someone to blame
He was left by the emergency doors
maybe for the whole world to see the light again
through the sliding glass
No no there weren't any exit signs
but there he was wrapped in white linen
and seaweed and hemlock
little furrowed pink face speaking in babble tongue
Some say black or yellow others brown or red
Depends on who you talk to
But with semi-automatic gestures
index finger raised pointing to the moon

explaining to the nurse
something she quickly forgot
God just disappeared vanished
without a government social security card
a driver's license or a gambling debt
Nothing ordinary to show he was mundane
but much more powerful than the rest of us
Twenty-one years after this urban legend
was told which still holds some ground
in the odd graphic novel
people forgot how to pray
wrapped in dysfunctional swaddle
of modern societal cultural misfitism
Rote material celebrations
continuations of vacuous holidays
eviscerating spirit-imbued ceremonial prowess
Now well-now they all prattle on about
mask or no mask while everyone's wearing a mask
The weather and taxes, terrorism, ecological collapse
gender issues, species decimation, the goddess
and new age illusion, delusion ad infinitum
All valid reasonable yes yes but the cure…
The sacred medicine was not here and it wasn't
glorifying the demigods, Big Head, Bullion Head
Possessions Head or exalting our next president savior
Game of Thrones wonder or dream house ambition
Folks step outside in nature these days
and it's like visiting another planet
Out of reason we have gotten out of season
But then Mary showed up thank God
No not the Christian Mary you're thinking about
But some pagan like Cailleach
like an old bizarre herb smelling lexicon
Old fruit that wouldn't bruise
die or change color
She just pointed at the moon
And people started getting it - presence

They started feeling different - awareness
Watching the light cool sphere
suspended in its blue shadows
surrounded by stars
Clouds passed across their vision
They tried swiping them away like flies
Their transfixion was an osmosis
of embodied sentience
Their hearts felt lifted and torn
by the long absence of moon, now returned
moon was the feminine side of God
The light of God's love-eye reflected
And God was a child but not a man
God was a goddess urchin who was hungry
for real prayer real purpose
real earnest and honest commitment
to commune or she would not play
She'd just run off, wander away
Maybe show up again
in say a stable or a supermarket
on the keyboards of a computer even
Or just lay there on the moon
waiting for us to get our shit together
Make life holy again
at least start making it respectable
And have some reverence
for the earth her cousin
And certainly have care and reflect
on what moves in and out of your circle
And damn it love and respect the animals
and trees and waters and all elements
And I told this story to children God's age
and they saw the truth in it
Why can't we

God is an old woman now
most people don't recognize her

hardly considering the old anymore
But she came back into town with a circus
for what was to be the last show
Everyone knows how kids like a circus
and most begrudging adults too
She set the three big tops up overnight by herself
under the waning moon
When the show started she ran through the three
rings on fire and got everyone laughing
She told the lions to challenge the adult ticket buyers
a little fear to find their courage
She had the seals throw the haughty
popcorn throwers out
And let the penniless urchins sneak in
past scary clown sentries (without painted faces)
She kept to the big tent at night
alone when everyone went home
She used the tent pole as an axis mundi
the blank white canvas to sail through the stars
Many dreamed of her that night
cackling like a witch through the solar system
Creating new worlds in her wake
until the modern world chopped down her pole
The next day, you couldn't hear anything
but a raging storm after that, for the rest of your life
And here we are at the end of the story
but there's still hope

Because of how she used that sail at night
when most were sleeping
She had collected all those big-hearted thoughts
and gestures of ours in a grocery bag
Poked pin holes in it for us to breathe freely
as she hung it on the top branches
of the green holy tree, a living gift, shining
through all points in the world
Leaving footnotes for slow learners

and cradling the young in secret tongues

SHAKING THE VISION BRANCHES

1.

I the one-legged lord of windy mists
and boreal borderlands
skilled in the permutations of coarse shadow rot
bleeding into perception
send my serpent lightning leg down
splintering all banal exhausted forms
I sear, purify and seal the thinly controlled
madness into twisted wood
With ritual care I toss the deformations
into the chaos of the cauldron
cooking fire of cackling old women
wearing young women's masks
whisking their vision branches into smokescreens
confusing all boundaries

With vulture feather scalpel
and obsidian ritual knife I sever
and cast curing invocations
into the lost children of the stars
Hardened formations of thought bubble up
from their frozen bodies of light
With the dark loam of my voice
I sing bardic dreaming rites
through the moving earth mirror
sapphire veins, ammonite eyes
solar letters moving a wooden bookmark forward
through flood, fire and shelving ice
Elder voices, ceremonial places
in the stained-glass eyes of hooded crow

I sing this exalted ode to the wild mother
snow-cap breasted, corn-hair whorled

with hag stone throat warbling new lifelines
into her phantom palms of smoky quartz
with fiery star markings

I shake the vision branches further out
tumbling shale and sacred letters from an altar
Suspended on a crumbling ledge I pitch
whistles and tiger bells into the rock dharma
Mix bitter herbs with juniper and tobacco breath
blown over the monochrome of modernity's
unconscious descent, resuscitate the many selves
The not I, and the other within

2.

Squat vessel, skull and tail entwined
through the ribcage sieve
Changeling wrinkle in torso and snout
stiff clear whiskers
For forty-seven years
I apprenticed with nocturnal animals
Our sojourn rendering me invisible
to most human tribes

Ardent intrepid, ruminative initiate
watching the small flame of my mind image dance
in animal colors of hermetic seclusion
With honed quiet attention I would come to know
the twelve harmonically related overtones
for wrestling the myriad malignant spirits
filling the empty pages of inner traditions

I became like the winged tigers
of mystical owl societies
a werecat that would rise like the Sidhe at dusk
Known for my dealings with the death prophets
rapacious ghost hungers of polarized minds

sanctioned and ruled by empires of the same
I retrieved their brackish souls
wandering the winter sun's estuary
Otherworld, swirling eons of abrasion
falling stars of underworld thoughts
snared in torpid floating sedation
and gossamer gauze of indoctrinations

I drive a wedge of voltaic magic symbols
into the orbiting corrupt power
Sing ancestral songs into the mummified
Akashic records
disintegrating dysphoria

With soft-footed perception
I walk through the ritualized burials
of your bygone era
into this present moment
A hybrid sable beast
hidden in the midst of a dark pack
I raise my spine and ears
to the colonized burning winds
from the dark side of the moon crater
to vain human designs imploding Earth and soul
I track the vision and aural trails of all
that was denied or forgotten
draining light from your eyes

Your remaining salt and blood cinders
pass their cellular illumination
through the earth's marrow
bedrock birthplace of the green mother
seated at the right hand
of the breaking wave
crowned in bedewed grass blades
above your heartwood temple
She breathes new rhythmic life

into your suspended animation
ensouling children of poetry
with phosphorescent phonetics
mellifluous versifying ringing eternally
in waterfall-green consciousness

THE GLASS CONTINENT

After sacrifices are offered
to your prow-spirit at a storytelling ritual
you are named aloud and launched
Giant red star Alpha Serpentus
Your incandescent serpentine hull
with keel of volcanic glass
cast off, showering our lost cosmologies
before your genuflecting bow
Old Worldeater
born of ancient wind-fire and rolling tide
in your dying wake
summon scintillating waves of apotropaic magic
to crest over the frozen head-lands
Permeate the continents
ignite neoteric myths
from the brine of the sacred wound
to the coast of meditation

2.

Lost sun shards flare in her frozen
wake bob and sink
sailing backward with eyes longing forward
becoming a distant light on a grain of sand
the spreading seafloor grates witch bones
tusks, amulets, wands, crucifixes
a dead fertility goddess surrounded
by an unnourished vapor of prayer

Shimmering beneath the water of her eyes
a thin line of thought flickers
through the bulb of the hourglass
erratic glass platelets, time deposits
blue crystallized reflections pouring white

foam into habituated unbroken breakers
Could this be the blackhole pierced
at the end of her long sentence
letting the sharp-angled alphabet go down
to turn back the world's darkening tide
to rekindle a tear-full sea
with her lizardite effluvium

Her rainy wind voice and flint-scales
scintillate ebullient hydrothermals
through the lost and tangled nets
Harbor seals cry and dead lava gulls rise
auguring the fall of the people
who stole the pearl
severing the earth's mantle
grinding nature into money
through crooked jagged maws
Skeletons living outside their bodies
soft tissue sacs rapaciously eating
what they trail behind them
sifting through their own detritus
tearing with insatiable shadow-teeth
the life-engendering anomalous metaphors

Will we walk weary, barefoot and resolute
through the earth's wounded memory
with elegies for the alchemy of wisdom
with medicine words that make the body sing
in re-storied images, harmonic consonances
poetic croons for love, healing and totemic resurrection
through the crossroads of sword
ghost flower and poem
Will we resuscitate the old dead in this fifth season
Resurrect their pneuma from molecular clouds
within our conjoint wound
opaque density and senescence
pregnant with concealed fear

Our pillars of creation are filled
with the drowning silence
of words felled from nature
riven from beauty, disembodied from soul
until our body breaks the spell's artifice
by opening our senses to the earth
giving ear to her imaginative sound-scapes
Honeybees call us through
the leaf hollow of the soul

3.

If we don't sow inside our garden
the seeds inside us will rot
Ferment from the washed-out colors
old energy-releasing shadows lighter than death
metabolize the authentic weight of life
Everything is annulled in the vacuum
turning individuality and attainment inside-out
to redress the Narcissus syndrome
to fathom, salvage and bless the communal epicenter
with the naming and manifestation
of life-giving seeds, pansophic chants, title tracks
Holy Clown Suture and Trickster Antidote
rhythmic gray-haired songs buried beneath the earth
Each song a scattered rune map of mystical verse
a holy dictionary of light-filled words
illuminating our alliance with the mythic dance
with terra firma and stellae maris
Sun dancers and shadow eaters
Death healers and cloud nomads
Wind grapplers for the bird whisperers
incline our head to the wandering stars -
votive ships, she whom I speak of
is the night, turning into a crow
scrawling moon ink for the elders
piercing dream instruction -

to consecrate the emptiness
of this unknowing time
While gazing at the mollescent darkness
watch the emerging butterfly change
the color of our thinking
remembering lost parts of us
dreaming in the sanguine time warps
The shape-shifting Sidhe of many worlds
sail through the suspended elements in our plasma
writing holy words on our cell walls
Soaring birds know and feel how this can feel
The altar of being lies everywhere
Let the Titan mother crouch inside us
with her animal body filling
our sleepless luna eyes with primal sounds
drawing us inward
she wants us to cross the open
space without fear
The fierce nature of her love
is known by the edges of me
passing through the ley lines
feeling the silent breeze of her awareness
Deer goddess bursting green
from the inside out, morphing
into salt, insect shell, propolis
adder's-tongues, maidenhair ferns
Red deer of the flaming earth
horned branches bellowing
sky shale, hammers -
tree roots into the clouds
of the mind's empty plain
A stag reflecting on the beauty
of long sounding desire
To burn and not be consumed
To be consumed but not burned
as an unwritten page of light
as a numinous ideogram of paradox

multiplying in mythic prefigurations
A hibernating holy bear unearthed by revelation
grunting deep-throated hairy dreams
of resurrection from dust
of fear and fear not
The spirit mammal's
soul mending palpable dream images
They live on Earth under the moon's shadow
trembling eternal on the filament
of a spider's spiral web
slowly changing our stagnant
deep-rooted, overwrought patterns
with their mass, charge and spin
Shimmering constellations of power
A wild terra incognita penetrates the impasse
of stalled consciousness in the frozen calendar
crystallized lizard psychosis in exodus
Leave your bodies to enter the diaphanous voice
unearthly possessed cry of the shaman
with a coyote's quivering energy
on the living room floor
disordering the artificial over-domesticated
The seismic stanza breaks
the intangible taproot
of our corrupted artifacts and tropes
Worn to the spine of artifice
the listening leaf propels
from branch to branch
to humus on the bluff

4.

I wait in a time capsule to hear
the deer sound in fallen snow
In seven generations they will dig me up
to find ritual smoke plumes
in the black absence of swan

Crow on black wire rants of trees gone missing
Skeleton moon merges with voracious dawn
bleeding into abandoned sacred places
Forgotten naming invocations are somewhere
in a book now or in a swaying pine
touching a river current through wild grass
wind of a lush mountain mind
pollinates pine seed in the pineal gland
Animal tracks pursue
the hidden peak's dolmen voice
guides the ant carrying all
perforated dreams on his back
talking all syllables at once in a potent bestiary
In the wild courts of its underground portal
I see avian eyes of rose-colored moons
Each blink reveals a new life we've waited for
For light years I have fed this flying red serpent
to help me beyond personal design
My small hand by her vast eye
her feathers would like to be stroked by rainbows
Her beauty bonds with every good thing
I have ever done, with so little time left over
and everything just begun
When I am the dead phantom revelator
in the deranged winter times
of the humanoid future
these words will remain as buds
attached to our most tender branches
their spreading shelter
will inhabit the earth's
composted cosmology
dip inward and you'll feel
their poetry bloom inside our shared skin
and know you're carrying the dream
closer to the dawn's-light-home

WE THE PEOPLE OF THE TURTLE

In the beginning of our Turtle Cycle
Turtle sounded like an amphibious gurgle
Initiatic descent of a healing psalm
plumbing for lost souls
losing their light
in the infinite unconscious
Turtle swims through the stellar remnants
of our gravitational collapse
with the spiral arms of a rotating galaxy
Inward to dark rift and out to brighter worlds
migrating from dissolution to animation
Turtle sees its atavic reflection
in the unblinking eye of darkness
shimmering Saturn rings and floating stones
Fragments of magnetic north drifting
in petrified trance, globular clusters
littering the carapace shield
scorched armor for comets and asteroids
Turtle created the world
and the Turtle is the word
And the word comes reverberating
through its shell of divination
our domed mirror
as we build upon the mirror
walk upon the mirror
of the first word
which is the world
in all its forms

In the beginning was the downbeat rhythm of Turtle
churning the sea of material existence
And depending on how you look at the pulsing word
in its prescient infinity loop, you might perceive
our myriad moving things in cold-blooded

discordant harmony, ghost shells seeking life
in a mirage of pressured shallows
null hyper-surfaces
of the dualistic mind
Look deeper and we descend
through the inflated self-world
into the bottomless expanse
of our Avatar Turtle's incarnation
her mystical utterance stirring
a spiritual regeneration of the multiverse

Swamp-pond snapping turtle expanding water rings
rock the water lilies and snow-capped peaks
With patient sapience and trust we keep
sacred bonds to the turtle beak mandible's
mythical expression behind our modern thoughts
Speak blue-green colossal turtle
through our innermost lives
We who are in covenant
to your claws and snake head
your green dinosaur tale's
Re-creation story
bubbling up to the surface
echoing memento mori
from the undulating kelp forest
Breath releasing clear Atlantean globules
between tin cans, tires and plastic life
Aboriginal pilgrim moving
slowly in internal reflection
through land-veins and sea-trance of merfolk
Tortoise stalking the tree of souls
silver pollen trails blown off course

Reverence for those who can see turtle
those who can hear its dance in the moving word
and metabolize its legendary meaning
Once no one would dream of eating turtle

but it is happening now
Her deific word is disemboweled
Her moon eggs are getting dimmer
growing gray in our thoughts
Predators claim her savagely
tracks to her wild story are blurred
manipulated into aberrations
Farmers imprison her
as delicacy for the living-dead

Turtle who teaches the soul I Ching and the Tao
Turtle who lights the winter campfire stories
to bring relief and instructive sacred knowledge
Mnemonic retelling of the wise turtle who is smarter
than restless empty satisfying of quick needs
Clever enough through the millions of years
to keep rising through our capricious
forms and fixed ideas

Turtle of the deep and quiet word
translucent nature linguist
crawls with her belly close to our earth
smoothing the original light out of stone

Then swims our omniscient theater
leaving nocturnal poetry in her wake
webbed foot in our blood pulse
divining the direction of well-being
Even when we get lost in our cunning
casting shadows ahead of us
Turtle will not retract her neck
or slough us off her protective back
She consecrates our quest for self-realization
banishes the diamond lizard angels on our backs
with her genius, Turtle is, and will be, the last word
resurrected from our empty ears and omega breath
Turtle words float in re-enacted song-images

in the hallowed holy water inside us
coursing through our infernal nether regions
through mineral and frost stars in our aureola amulets
they carry a community of awakened lives to her altar
Our collective presence follows
a common blood upriver
to the first light's desire for Tortuga courtship
We the people of the turtle seeking turtle life
wander through her Bedouin tent flap
flapping its flipper
Inside we discover terrapin fidelity and rapture
tunneling through the mountains inside us
climbing the ladder of moonwort fern
moving to the light of the first turtle word
forged from stars collapsing dust inside and out
We feel her first birthing stones
and pools of water spiraling
spiraling in the clay of our body and in zodiac wheels
of gypsy carts filled with deepspace
Together we follow her tracks with travois axis poles
dragging fields of time through sky-signs
we return to the present moment
to a self that once existed as a butterfly
filled with suns from the golden ratio
In the mushroom spore
germinated from hidden geometries
we spawn more nights for fox shrill and guttering
we weave more day for the winged bee maidens
oscillating neoteric azure mirrors
to magnify and regenerate the lifeforce
From turtle smeared words in wet primordial eggs
we crack open and cry up her ancient wonders
into the fairy full sky inside the World Turtle

THE COSMIC HUNT

I lived here a year before I was born
under the earth inside a malachite stone
an unresolved star from the galactic plane
I lay the memory crag of my azurite forehead
across the unraveled hypnotic centuries
Chronicles of myself after the extinction
sweating through the mountain's backbone
dispersing bohdi seeds, aboriginal words
infinite instances, benevolent zodiac
specter emissions

Spirits from the hinterland
enter my feathered headdress
They coo through the sinkholes and scree
click clack clattering
entering the culvert of my navel
beached whale of my heart drum

I drag my avian leg behind
attempting to learn more of our future
in the undergrowth
To heighten senses
I turn the fluorescent beetle right side up
and disappear into bird language
Speak of things I don't know
with refugee words from the dying
world's conscriptions

I speak of hidden moments in the birdhouse
Cloudy ignitions of vernal longing
I hear the minute engines in liquid iron
Crowded voices fading in collective wounds
"We were cleverly ensnared
in the dead matter of the world

Vainglorious we showcased ourselves
with intrepid malignant excess
We devoured our holy alliance
effacing our human - nature relationship
Swallowed our self and each other
inside the belly of the beast"
I inscribed
"Undertaking the soul's mythical quest
became a lost calling"

Swirling ghost voices enter
our post-modern spectacle
supplanting spiritual yearning
with suffocating self-importance
Wisdom of our indigenous taproots
vanish beneath the ground of our being
displacing cultural sageness
to remote corners of the earth

Narcissistic automatons regurgitate zeros
babbling in autogenetic succession
An underworld is created
on the surface of the planet
condensed behemoth clouds
stand petrified between our false fronts

The wind beats the green skin
of the pathfinder's plaintive drum
syncopating offbeat time signatures
in dark and light timbre
Musical colors perfume the ear
of the great mystery arouse
effusive poetic bilocation
out-of-body gnosis
of the underworld fates
Summons sonorous
latent downbeat strokes

inside subterranean ceremonial rooms
quickening vegetative constellations
for the liana spirits to open up the ground
for the return of the living dead

The future of humanity will make sense
if I keep cultivating the bloom
of our entwined roots
germinated from synergistic star patterns
If I hunt out the remains of symbiotic sanctuaries
from our celestial origins
If I keep ahead of the dimming consciousness
cultivating its maundering incoherent abyss
If I curate the residue of light
between you and your shadow
If I can transcribe the ambient acoustics
from the carbon of the Creator's rhythmic breath
before it goes silent with its names
and presences of sacred beings

Inspired by a true story
the Machiavellian movie plays
at the theater of distractions inside us
shrouds the brilliant asterism designed
when our first names were given
inside the aurora of the upper atmosphere
Obscure film clips of forgotten destiny
sink into what's left of postmortem inquiry

I cut bite size pieces of manna from caches
of timeless time and inner light
and offer them to the autonomous rebel bird tribes
I record how time operates turning over and over
inside its skinny nest in the changing
eyes of my green swarthy fey feline companion
I unscramble dragon riddles for her stray cat peoples

Bear with me while we wait
for the dead season of black moons
and square clouds to be undermined
by our patient prayers wreathing
She purrs rainbows for the mother ship
refracting fractal prisms
for the new dawn to unwind from oblivion
Rise from the underworld
Enter the daydream spectrum
tongue-clicking echolocating
translucent red fairy snail operator
arching the otherworld threshold
to guide the hellcat's soul parachuting
through feint hungry birdsong
under the empty birdfeeder
We sway together as weeping
winter rain as willows
feeling the quick of our wildwood seed
I command a host of heaven's armies
Cherubim with winged bodies covered in eyes
cross the vault of the sky
chanting mellifluous mantras
simpatico symphonious peace peace peace

Gaming crows mock this absurd melodrama
with artless aerial acrobatics
sharp and biting caws reeling
over the sky-scraping
wind-turbine canopy
I travel faintly redolent air currents
cutting through the dark-winged trickster cult
Beaks and talons thrash and fade in my wake
as I plunge headfirst into the deep garland mirrors
Great mother of all water spirits fierce and alluring
undulates her flowery headwaters
so that I may see my many selves
in every direction luminous

Whitecaps lunge and topple
in turbulent deaths they disperse
and rise again with light-bearing up-surge
from the cold spiritless deep
The perished reach through spraying foam
from reanimated ions in dissolution
their long shadows flash and flare
in blood and salt arcs
Anamnesis in the ouroboros
I press their leader's conch-trumpet to my cochlea
gleaning from its aural primordial memory
visions of fallen angels riding black
seahorses over briny crests
creating whirlpools and nautilus spirals
through the surface of our lives
We can still feel their churning
Can we save the ones who drowned
out their calling to navigate the soul passage
I submerge in the squelches deafening cry
to refashion their ancestral bones
and find myself in the liminal half-light
of a megalithic court-tomb
Cave bear presents herself
as gatekeeper and guardian
She asks if I have returned
dry as a bone and puzzled
from the same meteoric dust
that took her family away to another world
Thinking quietly on how many worlds there are
and the aqueous one I was in moments ago
we watch flickering shades
of smoky torchlight
change our appearance
I become bear, bear becomes me
then I become human-bear
and she becomes bear-human
I turn my attention away to the crystal stalactites

and tell her I don't know if it's enough
to be a mystagogue anymore
speaking in tongues to my human family
scattering mystical words
of complex beauty to renew
the sacred mysteries
Was it my fate to become
a divergent bardic contortionist
who utters the talus into tectonic thrust
whose doctoring finger-mallets retune the pitch
of xylophonic skeletons and their uvula resonators
back to clear harmonics
Bear shrugs while staring at the fire
having already served her part
in the space-time continuum
Her body language pours through me
roots, berries and bee stings
melted silvery warm snowflakes
tinkling raw honeycomb particles
cascade into my adrenalin stream
Ravenous and wild from long hibernation
I leave she-bear to hunt the koans
of torn angel wings fluttering
in abandoned mineshafts
I ponder turtleshell divinations
in their slow arterial walk
through cattails, tidal grass and rubble
See the old diamond miner words
wedged in an open cut and return
their glaring hardness to the darkness
where they were birthed
Dig deeper for the soul's profundity
I echo through the layered pit
you who severed yourselves from nature

THE WISE ELF

I came to meet Alfred
through the unbridled guidance
of two Shetland pony colleagues
I used to traverse the spirit-plain with
Maybe you have heard of them
Coauthors of Indigenous Earth Wisdom
and its Cosmological Intelligence
They gave me a neigh and nod
towards the wee hilly copse
behind our faded thrift cottage
It was here I found Alfred leaning casually
against the oldest rowan tree not yet berried
Alfred's symbolic surname is Old
English for Elf Counsel or Wise Elf
He wasn't the type to suffer fools lightly as they say
Or so I was warned by my pensive pony companions
Those who were quick-witted enough
to capture his charged runic utterance with mindfulness
felt they had just magically acquired
the relished words of a ghostwriter's dream
and immediately rushed off to create
movie adaptations for the art-house circuit
Leaping forward over a protracted chimera of time
I vaguely recall Alfred agreeing to mentor me
Mine was a deep purr of a large feline fully sated
as I felt my indecipherable dreams being fused
to a hidden resurrected narrative within
Alfred's Store of Talking Skeletons
(A shop where he kept all finely ossified
mineral rich bones of humans he thoroughly knew)
An alluring secret was that ONLY the unconscious
skeletons were ever sold as decoys
These were thin dimwitted skeletons
but profiled as exotic commodities in limited edition

This was not a con but a paradoxical strategy
to target greedy global leaders
entice them with highly lucrative payoffs
complete with a rallying slogan, the usual spin
"This osseous matter is good for the economy"
A ploy misdirecting the corrupt and unhinged
powerful people all over the world to buy
the inflated brainless bones as rare artifacts
The store's revenue was then secretly channeled
back into consciousness-raising efforts
The locals were horrified by this garish commerce
but Alfred artfully alchemized
the most elevated fashion
and outrageous trend of our times
Most skeletons were bought for their glamour
rare vintage hats with large black feathers
and burnished oval beads that twinkled
and dangled from cervical vertebrae
Transaction agreements clearly stated
"NO select parts would be sold
for totemic or fetish usage"
Buyers were required to purchase the whole corpus
This protected the more deserving people
from having a chance to be hoodwinked
Of course the instant these uncanny undercarriages
rolled out of the storefront they would refuse to talk
Rumors said they could but even under grave
threat all remained silent

Note: for the record
There was never any protest
or buyer's remorse over this
Just acquiring a numbskull obviously improved one's
material and social status by great class-leaps
This gave a magnificent counterfeit sense of power
to the ego which would diminish over time
requiring another impulsive purchase

to sustain even a modicum of fleeting happiness

Our living bones we kept to ourselves
These talking skeletons were dignified
and wholly reliable in these darkening times
They were powerful and eloquent ancestors
that we clung close to in reverence
As Alfred's protégé I sat in the midnight
ceremonies with this liminal council
Both eerie and comforting at the same time
their very presence changes you
Under tutelage I recorded
some of their rapturous orations
Later Alfred made me the executor of his will
imparting all-inclusive rights
to divulge our mystical praxis with the bone talkers
"Deliver these oracular words to the public" it says
"with any editing discretion you find necessary
It is time at this critical juncture
for Earth's inhabitants to know their sunset"

And as with any ancient but living sacred story
you are meant to see yourself in it
For healing and transformation
let the acoustics of its vowels and consonants
slip through your defenses
These stories were born long
before literary devices like subterfuge
Skeleton parables have their own inherent designs
I have added a short biography for each entity
and for the record the following
was told to me directly
and has been left entirely unedited
so the listener might experience
their integrity with visceral immediacy
and carry the piercing energetic surge
of retelling light to brighten the blackening hour

The moment I would rest my fingers
on their blanched phalanges
the bone-talkers would begin to tell me what
should be known in our world
Their dialogue may sound
like seductive spellssssssss
sciomantic, sibylline, sui generis sssssss
but I believe this discourse to be very insightful
and vital to our survival
I have given the birth names of each skeleton
along with their etymological names
Stay loose, ponder carefully, quietly, slowly digest
The reward will be spine tingling

Althea (The Healer)
"Resurrect my old holy hands
Slide them along your lifeline
Feel the sacred meaning
in each wrinkle of time
I have an old mountain to grow
slowly slow to make my future ancestors glow"

Althea has a posthumous book of riddles
titled Day Dreams in a Desert Cave
Out of print now for being written in ancient Sanskrit
it is in fact a map of divinations from the Gnostics
Channeled by Althea during her last year on Earth
it resides in a broken vault
in the basement of a Brooklyn library
Police breaking and entering reports
state modus operandi found inconclusive
No arrests were made
Forensic reports note Arabian
Desert sand by the vault door
Facilities manager statement
claimed the basement "is notoriously haunted"

Ivagenos (Yew Tree Born)
"I have ridden the hidden energies
Shell currencies of Africa
Brass bells of ceremonial horses
I have seen the Tree of Life re-grown
from the mystical mist gardens
of primordial Buddhas and Madonnas"

Ivagenos is known for his wild eccentricities
He once quaffed white hot candle wax with us
present and attendant to his radical needs
He then spewed a green mist with a world
in each globule back into the dancing flicker
Like a circus act gone bad he self-ignited
but from the midst of the erupted flare
transpired a cantillating instructive ritual
From the flickering verdant image
we saw our lucent eternal selves
with a pagan wisdom we had yet to fathom
until the light went out in his silver moss eyes

He was once an instructor of chaos
at the Massachusetts Institute of Technology
but his illusionary feedback loops
and controlled random disorder
undermined the confidence of his factional colleagues
refusing to adapt to his unnerving visions of chaos
Ivagenos was harangued shamelessly
with futile false accusations up until his last
jaw-dropping disappearing act

Gatteglan (Wise Pure One)
"I have carried invisible baskets of hives
and lightning into the crowds of clouded fear
To awaken your soul's pattern of being
I have resurrected the multifaceted crystallite
of all my unmined thoughts

I draw out the smoldering darkness
from burning empty pockets of the dead"

Gatteglan worked in the Peace Corps and Red Cross
until she got tired of the politics
She then removed herself from the world
becoming a usurper of the corrupt façades
of democracy and socialism by hexing
oligarchs and autocrats
Remaining true to her reclusive nature
allowed this wild hermit plenty of time
to expand her formidable creative talents
Paradoxically her reputation grew by default
Her shards of poetic justice and weavings of wisdom
were hurled at uncooked trespassers
Baffled by her rude genius
word spread quickly
and as more and more uninvited
approached her humble cottage
she would howl such haunting noises
in unison with her pet coyote
that all panicked, froze, then fled terrified
with their poor attention spans distracted
into new cosmetic abstractions
of myriad fleeting anti-cultural trends
of narcissism, vanity, popularity and fortune
fantasies void of cultivated spiritual values
and perception slanted by ideological
prosopopoeia pontificated by political
propaganda machines polarizing the factions
into mocking each other
with a cacophony of schisms
creating popping sounds inside all hollow skulls

Lost in this materialistic consumer trance
their transfixed glaze of petrified vision
brought a dissolution of vital holistic values

releasing toxic thoughts into the atmosphere
and into each other, begetting the same…
Gatteglan was completely forgotten about
until now at this 25th hour

Barnabus (Son of Prophecy)
"My testimony has been corrupted
by half-listeners
The chasm between us is filled
with dull knives and hidden serpents
I have gone back to leaning
against the window of my vision
The path tilts into boundless design
The rusted chain washes away
My vessel moves through the looking glass
into the crisp thin distance
I am like a guest of myself
It's too late for words about existence
They have all traveled too deep inward"

Barnabus was a fully tenured professor
an esteemed philosopher of our parallel universe
A deep linguistic thinker unmatched
in his depths of ponderous thought
he would spend years studying
the curved and angled shapes of a morpheme
and the sonic ancient history of the word's origin
tracking through natural history
and humanoid liminal states all the way back
to its fragmented primeval utterance

Barnabus had an earlier stint as a merchant mariner
and rode the rails during the depression
During the dot com boom
he sent gift crates of apples to various CEOs
They were stolen from Eden

Amaterasu (Shining Over Heaven)
"Oh Grandmother Moon
I sweep and sweep
the pearl black surface of your eye
your reflection of warmth underneath
the light of rust dark chimneys lies"

Amaterasu was an obscure but gifted
mythopoetic conjurer and mystical storyteller
for those who died early in life
and those who sought the trials of the sacred gauntlet
She never wore her tribe's traditional dress
and preferred traversing snowy peaks
to search for caves where the old gods still dwelled
Once inside the cave's mouth
she would turn into a bat whose claws gripped
late autumn meadow flowers as an offering
to the creatures of the underworld
The floral perfume exuded lost love and restorative care
appealing to the discerning but sentimental empathy
of the fearsome, awe-inspiring zoomorphic beasts
Her renown in these realms
has not seen the light of day
which she prefers

Branogenos (Raven Born)
"Your habitat is not yet gone
My pillaged messages still cling
to the clicking and chattering of trees in the wind
From furnaces of the oldest lightning strikes
rekindling life from a world gone dark and cold
my fulgurite words will be exhumed
as signal fire utterance above the burial grounds
I am the immortal numinous syllable
perpetually chanting the sage intimate undertones
as sonic insight to sagacious seekers
the resilience of *nature* and your nature

The frenetic energy of rebirth
in the hibernating death ode

I am the formations of luminescence
in the pigment of your skin
Curl cresting into the universe
in ecstatic abandon
I am the undercurrent of unheard holy words
between words never spoken
but perceived and lived in the breath"

Branogenos never talked about himself
but was mesmerizing in conversation
People would often comment that his words
would administer overdoses
of synesthetic anti-truthphobia medicine
inculcating an incorruptible integrity
He would project images of himself
as a deadly mantis in a giant bug movie
fighting a dragonfly to scare the fear out of you
or appeared in humanoid silhouette form
speaking in tongues to magnified protozoa
while quivering in a swamp surrounded
by poison dart frogs
Then Branogenos would leave in a flash of epiphanies
hypnotizing the unsuspecting intent listeners
who swayed shimmering and liberated
from their white static mind-mutterings
Rapturously slurred with egalitarian virtues
drunk on the sudden beauty
of his furious thunderbolt firmament

My new formidable assignment with Alfred
was located at a remote inaccessible site
where all our ancestors go to find recourse
from their most pressing issues
When I myself died, Alfred and I

served together at said gated outpost
With Alfred as the overseer
and Chief Council of the Dead
we received all newcomers here as well as old
We were never bored
always playing pranks on the newly deceased
So many of them confused you know
this was a way to lighten them up
help them see clearly, but we were tender too
for those who really needed it
Always busy we were helping people
return to Earth with renewed vows
and commitments to rediscovered spirit allies
We helped them redefine their roles
to address unfinished business
We were caring for fish and seaweed too
anthropoids, tree ferns - everything really
all kinds of nameless lifeforms I spent lifetimes
learning their languages
I was captivated by entities
from whom no discernible sound
or sign was emitted like communing whales
without sonar singing or body language
These translucent beings that few could see
carried a spiritual vapor in the breath
exhaling the essence of novel length information
transmitting vivid images of the past
present and future invisible to the human eye

Anyways, space is opening up
Alfred and I are soon to retire
and if you are one of the chosen few
to have read this far along
you might be interested in applying
for work at the outpost
Send alpha brain waves signaling your interest
without personality projections

perplexing dream transmissions
or emotional distortion
You must communicate clearly
then we will know
whether you're ready for the next step
or still perpetuating the inflated ego
You will also need to triangulate yourself
and provide your grid reference
along with the oldest ancestor's
name that you know
Include which tree and what landscape
are your favorites
Then address your mind
to the seventh soul organism
We are waiting here
Deadline is sooner than you expect

FIRST DEAD SHAMAN OF THE UNIVERSE

The first dead shaman of the universe
floats in moon silvers, flower songs and birth cords
I am inside him, while still here, and nowhere
surrounded by images resurrected from a dead world
Threads of me drift through his astro-apertures
two yellowing moon orbs
transmitting sinuous visions
from his colossal dream skull -
thoughts covered in first frost
lungs of rain bellowing high wind
over wildfire rumination
lush and shadowy vegetation
toppling in landslide revision
Between the lines in his palms
stars and souls
orbit each other in mating flight
Five rays from his hybrid bones
shake open afterlife distances
elongating landscapes of liminal space
mirrored islands in stellar seas of the heart

Like all of my kind I am hewn from deific origins
my portraiture was atomized in his mortar
Skeleton mashed into curing balm
for the sickness of the land, paralyzed beauty
lost covenants, hardened delusions
Lava rock pestle creating beginnings from ends,
sacrifices and reanimates the soul's
blinding opalescence
jolts clear-light sentences awake, sentient
bright clusters of sonorant word couriers
become allied arrows of aural Indian ink
running through the earth's transit zone
rhythmic script winding through the esker

journeying to the bones of a ghost buffalo
tearing along a plain, the laugh of a witch cornered
by the sun, her wolf reading a smoldering book
of baptismal water dissipating inside the anvil of the sky
Where moon glint meets disintegrating cloud
are the waiting daemons of spell-water
inverted from ice

Many I am's turning the earth into desert and flood
churning the wind into blind syllables
exiled cursive word temples into droning
circles of regurgitated axioms
Sleepwalkers puff and swirl their personalities
in the coliseum
I see their carbon copies with spectral fingerprints
still shackled to the dead seabed
Apparitions from their lampblack scrimshaw
scrawl are turning beluga gusts into maelstroms

Dead flying through smoke holes - not yet dead, not yet
inside bronze leaf litter, silt and fog they grow up
through beautiful accidents struck
from their silent guitar strings

Particles of self without antenna
or astronomical anatomy
Primeval creatures flying without wings
glance my eyes
Mastodons, scapegoats, black sheep, sorcerers
Fallen stars of angel teeth, scarred wolf wings
Ghost dogs in late night wanderings
inside the invisible massif
Seat of the dead shaman's soul

It can't be written, said or sung
what I've witnessed while apprenticed

to the muse-hive inside his exoplanet-cranium hanging
suspended, homeless, Adam's apple
still serving the grail, protects the vocal cords
of extraterrestrials calling to us inside our sleeping time

Feathered fire serpents will ascend
again from his sepulchers
harbingers for those who are bound to his precepts
As for the dead parts of us becoming the wilderness
I will speak no more nor portend
the world has fallen to darkness

When I am clear, a bell tolls at the crossroads
inside his apiary, rich resonant stings
of a healer's tongue probe the blank parables
Reflective compass needle penetrates
the soul's self-perpetuating eons

I leave behind this threshold-poem's cycle
to flutter your body sheath awake
with geomorphic medicine bundled lines
yin-glazed from amulet perception
garnered from my apprenticeship
with the last dead shaman of the universe

He is the last aboriginal monarch
masked as a Luna moth
cloaked in the moon's shadow he descends
splitting the pupa of subliminal night
passing rainbows into the swaying wake
of the whale I once was
marooned with my humpback songs
about melodious terraqueous beauty
filtering sunrise through each vaulting curve of bone
Identical shadows heaped on top of each other
silently cultivating symbiotic sapience in breath currents
the undertow of his shamanic pulsed calls

bleed into my changing shore
I am an ardent student to his articulate tides
heir to the in-surge of manifold beings
that push the cataract of serpent trance
and stored wild honey, out of my creaturely body

The azimuth of the shaman's undercurrent
weaves its dream shape inside me
spins alpaca wool and macaw feathers into headdresses

Spinneret-woven silk poetry threads
spread rainbow rain showers into gray films of reality
splash green tiger bell orbs over the stratified sand
peal into a corolla of bright colorful petals
Love blooms in the ascending aorta

And summons the holy tongue to speak within
and through unheard voices
forgotten names, abandoned peoples
emerge as ships passing in the night

Sail on iridescent pilgrims
shower your golden plumes
through devoured stars and razed hallowed gardens
bound for the sacred firs of Oyamel
within the celestial sea of the shaman's reflections
strike the flower head of our iron-centered Earth
Cultivate the sky god's nectar, know that I am
in you and you are in me
first dead shaman of the universe

THE FIRST LANGUAGE

Follow the incantatory image
and you won't be what you have been
accumulating an outer shell of personality
for the stranger while your polished light disintegrates
oscillating in random information particles
inside the top-heavy cranial cavity
You won't be
what you think you will be
in the future that doesn't exist
In the end matter and anti-matter
will take us all dead or alive
It already has, long ago
our maps blurred in the aeolian wind
The hemoglobin drifts in the prevailing
suspension of consciousness
cognitive dissonance caves into perceptible defense
internal combustion sputters into linguicide

Onward soporific shadows, molt!
Renew the ancient archetypes
from repressed interior worlds
Still you can breathe among our fading colors
of the headland among other things
Use the reflecting mind's eye to synchronize
the distorted rifts in perception
bending truth into misshapen reality

Sometimes you can see through
everything and see nothing
Or see through everything and see everything -
the original halcyon *light* spoken
the animate first holy words
articulated into the body
A flooding clarity of telekinetic poetry

in the house of ruin
Vestiges of beauty in the distance
between the seeker's thought
and sentient illumination
at the migratory edge of awareness
Follow the ethereal empty silent intervals
Shrouded presences between heartbeats
beat-beat
encounters with unseen shimmering angels
beat-beat
pulse in the crystalline cornea

When you speak you must pay attention
to the reverberations of primal
archetypes in your voice
When you drink make sure it's not red plasma
When you think try getting between
the eternal and temporal self
Listen more to the wildlife in your body
you have two ears for a reason
and only one mouth for an ardent reason
Articulate the passionate beauty of three swans
living under the lake inside a blue crystal stylus
leaking what we want to know
Lift and draw the deer breath on the shoreline
as it permeates the rainbow's sheltering
of the petrified she-wolf skull
Her lupus thoughts rest in the moon's refuge
she grows wild strawberries in her eye sockets
defies chemical poisoning
and reverses the word *time*
as cause of entropy - back to its original word *emit*
The reversal of the word *no* (as in time)
as in no post-existence is *on*
To turn *on* and *emit* the unobscured
memory of our dead language exhaled from nature
reverse the negative space

in the portal of the bell tower
by renouncing the angels of oblivion
Set the three swans free inside your mind
cleanse your poisons to become the fruit of life

The tree of life is a hybrid burning bush
its stunted flowerless limb sways
after the songbird leaves
Did you take notice of this
fluctuating bush language
flux of sound and shadow
across colorable reality
or is it just bird aftereffect
Now ask yourself
which is the most fitting living-limb to proceed
to perch alert and move on, go into orbit
What air is given to each direction
What seed was shared to sustain life
What competitor moved the song away
What kind of observer is behind
the dilated eye searching
Why witness the voices of ancient peoples rising
Why give attention to this underground story
Are these my thoughts
or thoughts of the land disappearing
in binary nomenclature

My next two sentences fly bewildered
as a Tibetan antelope in a doctored photo
as a volcanic asteroid
lowering itself to the human world
My conspicuous words can be incarcerated
stalked shot caged eaten
I avoid carcasses when hunting for clean water
Is this my magnetic separation from true north
leaching acid run-off
If I should forget myself

I know you are inside me underworld raven
Your homes and gravesites
perched up and down my vertebrae
Your feathers still glued to my old nests
cracked shell dreams of acrobatic air
before the city-states slew wisdom
with their daemon breath
upon our withering branches

We dark-veined holy ghosts are reflecting
upon the surface of things material
comfort sinking slowly into empathic fracture
Am I one of these transient sightings
slowly consumed by the weight of the earth
But who am I if I am not these things I write
These street numbers squatting at intersections
These reeds messaging Morse through gray water
Wind-breath of the first language
cusp my identity to your storytelling
If I express your poetic nature
clear to the ear of my drum
will it illumine the rock faces of the stone peoples
If I feed it to the desensitized leaden bodies
in their gilded open pits
hollowed out soulless alien centuries
insinuating their eroded languages through our skin -
If I serenade the dark night of your pseudonyms
and sing of your hidden things to the unversed unsung -
will it change the way we see things
Will the listener marveling at the mountain
of their own thoughts ever be the same
or will they limp away
with vegetated minds of immunity
behind strangled garden disguises

Teach me how to be taught plumed creator
fledgling apprentice to your first language

SOLARIUM OF HEART TALK

Who watches this prophesized shipwreck
dying and dying again in the onyx of my ring
Who gives sacrificial offerings to live
and live again in our bird-like Earth-song
Circular rhythm thrum of swirling loops
a consonance of lazy hurricanes
leaning heavy against sea and sky
sinks chthonic blue into our ribcage
never to be heard from again

Curio seekers scour their cyan eardrum
for the carved wooden lady's
trapped holy voice in the swell of wave
I pick up ghost pieces of her shine
White foam of her mouth crashes
along my shore where she always resides
with her lightning toned phrases
curling back to polished bone syntax
Coastal twinned elemental
a reckless angel who thinks she had her wings
spread inside our cinematic memories
forgot who she was, a figurehead on a bow
before the throbbing expanse
searching the vanishing language
of untroubled hours

Primeval priestess in pale nimbus light
shepherd the oceanic surge of buried tears
groom the aching painted flower
to emanate out-of-body
and be more than colored
arguments from God

With the wafer of the full moon

tide - under your tongue
burrow down next to me and listen
leaflets blow inside this perishing body
Gather the gossamer connections
Listen like a plant in the drizzle
Place flowers in each other
filling the lost forest ground
of your troubled wooden hearts

This courting psalm's leafy outgrowth
will scatter like ponies in sheets of rain
A feral foal will stop by
the crescendos high leak
embodied in our milky way
abyssal time-spinning oceans
From where we thirst in our coiled diamond stillness
mountain chains break into holy songs
From where we were once without meaning
serpentis Kundalini rises sinuous from the sacrum
Watchers call to us from the Tower of Babel
Telluric voices unfurl from tectonic burial grounds
gathering us into nature's place of power
they make space for our true mind
in the mystical garden of the heart

THE INSURMOUNTABLE HEAD AND ITS UNLIKELY PASSIONS

Saint John the Baptist's heraldic head
with its peculiar Martian bioluminescent antenna
was full of grace, and a revolutionary influence
to Doctor Gray's anatomy studies…
It had no grinding neuron
emissions casting darkness into the earth
Riddles, myths and poems were raised
from its dead matter
Burnt books were dislodged
from its inert memory
As it was neither shrunken nor severed
one could cultivate flowers inside the skull
In excellent condition for phrenology readings -
an 1857 medical text revealed the head's
protruding frontal bone was made
from crystallized light, enabling the head to see
unlikely passions of darkness, consuming the void
begetting more of the same
emptiness ad infinitum
Reflecting off Saint John's
ivory black sockets
were images of lost souls
With uncommon devotional enquiry
Doctor Gray discovered the unusual
with every turn of the knife
To further complicate the mysteries
his medical exams note the
mandible is unhinged
but still strangely capable of self-
generating oracular divinations
Which it still proceeds to do
incessantly to weary
medical researchers, scientists

and escaping lab rats

None of the elements found
inside the various structures of the head
were created by supernovas
and its substance was not common
to the earth's crust
The head's energy was simply
not derived from our periodic table
The implications of these findings
are still being deliberated in the courts
and contested by insurance companies
The head's value was considered immeasurable
and underwriters were convinced of fraud
A web of intrigue surrounding the alien holy head
gave rise to an unethical market price value
for each of John's high-profile cranium bone
fragments being secretly auctioned at Christie's
Suspicions from the Justice Department
exposed collusions on price-fixing scandals
and prison sentences followed
All this typical plundering hoopla aside
you can appreciate the controversy
this has raised about the stellar origins of our kind
and how the almighty power of affluence
can purchase grace from smuggled artifacts
of sacred value for speculative investment
This brings me to my own consternation however
Will the carbon stardust in the lair of our heads
end up absorbing all the light
Though this be a page of light
from the last two centimeters of silence
in a far corner of the world
it has escaped the blind disinformation engineers
at the crowning point of their powers waning
So it behooves us to pay attention

It has been said by some authorities
that the first head came
from the soliloquy of a speckled egg
Others, that it came from a burning blue star
that later turned red with age
Who has the time to deliberate these things
if they were so inclined
But postulate with me for a strange flashing moment
What are the implications of having a head
Why even bother questioning our head
The below entry was discovered
in Doctor Gray's diary as a footnote
(we can't be sure if it's in reference
to Saint John's head)
"If the head is decentralized
it will be stable in its trajectory
Over-rigid struts cause stress cracks
Plasticity of its skin in surface contact with
harsh environments allows for greater mobility
of emotional balance and support."
Head - you are not enough
but you are everything
We languish in earnest distraction
Momentum spills away from us
It was my refusal at first to be
a head of anything at all
that started me questioning its purpose
Jungian research indicates that when heads
are lost most individuals
(as well as groups of people caught
in a collective contagion of illusory ideals)
look up or down to find their heads
as if to say where did I come from
how did I lose it
and where lie my answers
Few look sideways at themselves and can say
all is not lost to vanity and projections

Far away in the sinkhole of time
the unconscious unquiet gyre
of the head's conditioning
flails in its quick self-absolutions
begetting beheadings, of nexus and logos
as a solution to our current disturbing reality
Did you read the above carefully inquisitor

But all is not lost I think to myself
Uttering my imagine-nation through
the mythic constellation of alluring images
poeticized through disordered senses

I who am the other within you
who iridesces and descends
sojourning in other times and places
scintillating in pitch dark unnamable religions
fallow memory fields of ice gouging out a valley
and the valley's green memory of ice
disappearing and returning in other ways
We are the same interior of the dead forest
dreaming of our minerals - rising from depleted soil
to heal decayed roots and husks of etheric hearts
bound to the same primordial laws

If you can't make heads or tails
of what I'm saying here
put it on a platter for immediate action later
When you become ravenous
for sustenance you won't be so picky

Strange to be talking to your head
at length keen reader
Such is the way of the head
that has lost all questionable etiquette

The following passages are from the burned books

and dead matter of Saint John

"Wicked are the Lotus-eating heads
Their bathroom is everywhere"

"Blind is thee who climbs over
the top of other heads without looking
through the window curtains
of their own vertiginous heads first"

"Biting someone's head off doesn't account
for the victim's head being in a storm
cloud or any unforeseeable crossbones
behind the facial skeleton, also -
take into consideration
the proportions of the victim's head
in relation to the biter's jaw
Has everything been sized properly to fit
Has the biter made allowances for
any invisible serpents
around their prey's
cervical vertebrae"

"Woe to those who see the world in black
and white… that is your shadow
The gray is your light"

I am the hermit, the Major Arcana in exile -
purifying the alphabet's characters
from their internal phonetic injuries
that detonate our relationships
I learned to keep my head hidden
in a small hand-woven cloth
in a hand-woven basket
in a small undisclosed village
There it sits in a weaver's hands
keeping watch over other heads

spewing words that fracture and devour

Sometimes my head doesn't return
from otherworld scouting missions
I send out a search party with my feelings
by keeping them bright
When I capture the head's insurrection
I turn off the light
Everything that it takes in
becomes a banquet for uninvited guests
One by one I plot with each consumer
Misdirect them to their own heads
I'll leave my head to you when I'm gone
I have others, all are decoys for you headhunters
Oracular heads can be savagely misconstrued

The head can be caught
between worlds all the time
Such is the risk of traveling
a self-perpetuating distance
Lament those who lose
their head in the dark
for they have materialized
into possessed mad images
lost in the wraith's pleasure gardens
for they are the blue burning stars
that lost their way in the cold
Sometimes when my head returns
on its own recognizance
I throw white powder over it in the cellar
to see if it still exists
Will a strangely familiar shape appear
like a knoll in the arctic
or has it returned as an apparition
Shadows appear on the periphery
for I have caught my head playing
with a witch's bone

and have seen it parachuting
faceless like snow
through low air pressure
inside the sky's dome

Should I fall somewhere else
Ironically I don't remember
choosing this darker version of Earth
Prostrate before the insatiable dust
and principles of darkness
I cast my crown of light into the shadows
illuminating the lifeless *dead* of night

What's a head like this really worth
If it multiplied from purely natural growth
If it's incubated by solar rays
and starlight who's to say
Can we further its usefulness
Can it be used as an immured shadow
for the moon's hangar bay
or be a host for the spiny winged marsh thistle heads
parachuting cottony seed incognito
Your head drifts and continues to disintegrate
as you read this required reading
 - prerequisite for any unlikely passions
but yet my treasured thought particles
still linger for those who hunt for thinking
outside of their own daydreaming thoughts
and grasping my illusive cognitive mysteries
you make feasible headway into the insurmountable
head cult's cogitation, where all is veritable and pure
yet still irrational, impetuous, irreverent peace
Our venerated foreheads point to the horizon
with a natural lean to the natural world
For entering the unnatural fray
of the public world we conjure
a synthetic head to befit the norm

The artificial fibers cannot be sustained
for long periods of time by our sensitized bodies
The chemical synthesis would diffuse
though our membranes
For restoration we go headless for a while
in the privacy of our own homes of course
During our communal ritual functions
we intimately enjoy invoking our head
to reappear in any desired form
depending on our mood or need
To cultivate heightened awareness
one might choose an animal head
or an insect head for microcosmic vision
One might adopt an angelic head
just to be on vacation
while reconnecting to the Godhead
but deific heads are never chosen
for vanity or alluring aesthetics
These base mortal traits are not found
in the Cult of Heads, in this regard
we are beyond reproach

In our cult we can emancipate any imprisoned head
We can conjure it by plucking a two-string harp
tuned to the eccentric lost voice
of the suppressed heretic
whose kinetic breath is teleported
and used as a catalyst
to materialize and reform the cephalic molecules
How do you think I made your head appear
in the interstice between acoustic frequency
in this unlikely time and place curious reader
But here you are to acquire a harp like ours
Head off to the far northern climes
Find a singing tree
wearing a carven swan head
Ask for its services

with thanks, blessings and prayer
Add vegetable fiber to its shaping
and fasten it with deer thoughts
Place a pebble wrapped in horsehair
inside the body cavity to resonate
with the soul of the world
A verdurous woman will appear
when you pluck her from the mist
Wearing a prismatic waterfall tunic
and viny hair coiled with pastoral pipers
she'll instruct you on how it is tuned
to the heartstrings
and to the onomatopoeias
of surrounding nature
As difficult as this task may seem
no good deep work comes easy
nor are its gifts given freely
Some have asked how
I have kept my head for so long
My head has a low profile
It has never sought the throne

If my head is accused for its sentiments
I send it away to mind its own business
and riddle it with distractions
I incite myself to the nonsense of divine language
Strike it in the temple until I hear its bell ring
follow the reverberations until I become one of them
Only then will I know my head is one with my soul
which is no place at all but rippling out in circular
magnetic waves through space
Through explosions and wormholes
into other dimensions my head came from
another head and that head did too
Can you imagine the very first head
that came before all

Well I had a dream about it last night
It was a horse head wearing skulls as a garland
The fearsome nag was both executioner
and a wise compassionate being
under our collective sea of unconscious
I did the deep dive and brought it up
but I was worried what it might say
I was relieved when it told me
I am doing what I am supposed to
while wading through an infinity of heads
I keep a honed eye inside my own every day

If you think my head ridiculous
it's your own fault for thinking you have one
Mine is invisible and sated on the nights
when all the gods and goddesses reincarnate
Praise to the head when it dreams well
damn it if it doesn't have coffee and poems
If I bared my vulnerable head to you
you would say it's soft and small like a marmot
Pickled it is beautiful, the size of a sausage or melon
It has ostrich feathers displayed in cuneiform
Young antelope graze along
its sparse savanna crown
It is a bewitched head
beholden to no earthly laws
It finds sustenance elsewhere
in stoic moons and eggs singing
their speckled blue forms into being
Its soliloquy is heard in old pianos
that still look for a garden of vision in their keys
It is a ripe head ready to be picked
Indifferent as a stemless eggplant
on a moonless night
Stay with it if you want
to carry stones with mind control
to reshape your life after death

When the old parts of you have died
by making peace with opposing views
I'll allow you entrance to my head
and once you get through
my ramshackle parapets
where I have dismantled my head's
ghost life in the machine
don't you feel just like
any other small animal head
Don't let my head's hulking gait scare you
behind its death mask
Now don't you feel like yourself
when someone else is different
Don't you feel like you have more time
most all the time
Don't you feel the liminal atmosphere
and that makes you think
you are the wilderness
of the body's unconscious
or that your spirit double interpenetrates
myriad dimensions of the multiverse
to commune with other beings
including the disguised coyote god
who lures you into his unruly creative power
Divine trickster and benefactor of the people
I offer you my incorporeal head
to light your fire for those in the dark
Religions don't know who they are
without our heart-minds

I can intuit when coyote is about to stick
his head inside mine
but there's not enough time
to banish his lawless cunning
I feel the wild grip of a rhubarb bite
sharp on my sugarless tongue
ALL GOOD THINGS TO THE HEAD I howl

moon eyes shining fearful in the changing hour
barking irreverently from the body's
vibrating skeleton cage
at the desert apparitions
Worship my good rubber ears for the road you're on
- you'll need these blessed amen wafers!!
Pointy, giddy with comic relief
forgive me, but I'm sending law abiding messages
down your vertical turnpike to those
great fucking hairy knees
buckling backwards laughing
clown head askew from my shoulders
glistening snake oil curdled in my belly
All Hail The Misshapen Head I yell
insane as a loose cannon
unhinged from my insurmountable pedestal
Try to gain composure I plead with myself
before my undead gathering,
struggling to keep a lid on their distressing
unearthly perception of my clown head
rocking madly about with tears and saliva running
gaudy with green, blue and orange makeup
Glutinous eyes and teeth filling with colorful aromas
attracting scarabs and boll weevils to banquet
Keep the laughter going I hoarsely growl
at the insects choking and sputtering
Wheeze OFF WITH THEIR HEADS!
MOVE IT BUGS!
Eerily watching my haunted head roll off its perch
and tripping my guests just to see their eyes lurch
Let it be known this is a clown's world
crawling with delusions of grandeur
until the walls crumble and peace falls
silently over reality

Head you are a strange entity
but you are neither manikin, puppet nor doll

You reason with all probable solutions
for your rote existence
I refuse and oppose
all factory-made substitutes
posing as real heads
Beware of the heads of state
with their shortages on brains
building soulless estates
We have collected these ghosts
close to our soul
with all our compromises

Ironically we have to find ways to keep our heads
at a safe distance from infiltrating head cases
Our maturation deficit is alarming
wouldn't you agree
If you play in the personality cults too much
while pretending serious me
If you are emotionally defensive
about your position as king or queen

Raise your head up as an effigy
Fill it with straw and mice
Set it on fire while protecting the mice
This is a rite of passage into true adulthood
No longer will you feel separate
from all that exists you will be recognized
by those that matter
with modest silent partnership
Quietly now go about your business
making the world a better place to live

As for these digressive vignettes
they are a staple for our times
One should bear them in mind
throughout the day as you groom
nibble and mimic animal sounds

reshaping your life from death
Dismantle, scratch your way out
let your head fall from your vice grip
Sometimes you need to sacrifice
your head like in days of old
If you need punitive charges
brought up against you
call me judge
Maybe put your head on a pike
to scare your enemies
and warn your friends

Shrinking heads might be our only viable solution
Dried right by an open fire, stuffed with herbs
they could become fragrantly appealing
and used as scapegoats
But keep your head and be wholehearted
as half heads are actually worse than no heads
They compete with each other
in unconscious desperation
All heads are vying for attention now
and all heads are giving them attention
while vying for their own attention
- it gets exhausting
Ecological collapse seems imminent
with so many talking heads trying to get noticed
I wane at the parapets of my observation tower
Don't get me wrong dear friend
Although I am without a halo
I deftly don a conspicuous pious tonsure
Sometimes when the wind blows
it shapes like a nest
Throughout history we have likened
our head to an egg
This is a simple natural unrest
a desire to be hatched again
But apparently any head will do sometimes

I'm home in mind - mine I mean
But if you are uncomfortable in yours
there are many clever things
you can do for your head
Like put it in a hole
like an ostrich
until you calm down
Put your head underwater
like a beautiful hissing swan
Pull up your roots
and remember your baby head
blowing bubbles
Distract it!
try this…
NOW PAY ATTENTION
envision your head with an owl's face
Then the back of your head
is the back of a deer's head
The right side of the face
is a German Shepherd's face
The left side of the face is a hare's head
twice the size as normal
and a good boxer with a black eye
She spars with coyote when it's feeling wily
Such a peculiar head
is never annoyed by hecklers
It has godhead authority
and is not subject to inconsolable grief
Devoted patron of the arts
undivided in your attention span
if I ruptured your sense of reality
it's because your slanted vision
was in a bubble and about to implode
I make no apology as you know
questioning the Cult of the Head
is a punishable offence
for inciting civil disobedience

New laws have been introduced
allowing *individuals*... to patent their head
and sell shares of it on the stock market
Inflatable heads made with cheap labor
set this popular trend in motion
With little side effect you can send your head
to the following address to qualify:
Defense Department of Finance and Accounting
Your monetary evaluation will be returned to you
with a profile status report
along with a self-inflicted implant
of loyal responsibility to the Shadows
Gradually you will climb in wealth and power
among fellow social engineers
with heads of black ice melting revealing
heads that like to put their heads in others
and turn them the way they like
Apparently this is easy to do
(seems uncomfortable to me)
Heads come with their own instructions
if you bother looking
but most heads are shaped and directed
by the content of other self-serving heads
yet they still fabricate illustrious delusional identities
reproducing the same vain facade
Please pardon my jaded woes
but things will slowly change for the better
I think you intuit that too inquisitive reader
Nevertheless the head has been deemed unreliable
by the infallible authority and saving grace
of Saint John's the Baptist's heraldic head
Due to the mob-head's systemic deceptions
infesting countless other talking heads
talking to the self and others
it has become mandatory to have one's head
examined with powerful microscopes and telescopes
This will alleviate false incriminations

and the scapegoating of the vulnerable
Ambitious self-importance will be flagged
for further investigation
Privacy laws will prohibit you
from seeing your own test results

If all goes well, in the near future
no individual's head will be deemed special in any way
no longer will humans be subjected
to officious rhetoric, hyperbole or gaslighting
All this unnatural, habituated
and disconnected way of life
will become a part of the earth's dark past
Last night it was announced
The Department of Education and Commerce
had created a historical theme park
depicting humanity's disintegration and fall
from its evolutionary potential
Life-like figures were programmed
to shout at passersby…
"Look there's Godhead!"
"Multiwarhead Headquartered"
"Headmaster Beheader"
"My head is better than your head - sing-along!"

At the entrance a placard reads
"As a newfound thoughtful
honest people we acknowledge
our ancestors represented in this park
If you don't see anyone you recognize
from the family album
headshots are available at the film industry store
Be sure to stop by and have an effigy
created in your likeness as well
It comes with a website with social media links
Enjoy your short stay and someone will come
to take away any empty heads in the morning

You'll have one phone call and can keep any small
invaluable personal items with you
Thank you for visiting"

HER WORLD SWIRLING AROUND US

I am spread thin on dawn's fire blade
belonging to nowhere to no one
Not to myself or these myths passing through
disinterred from strange subterranean altitudes
Uninhabited poems hard on the wind
refract through pink glass trees
transparent galleries of an ancient sky goddess
filling the hull of my magic birch bark canoe
Seeking destiny in an unknown body
pulls the mind away to the will of nature
The remains of myself increase her etheric heart
disarticulated tree shapes and subsongs arise
Tomorrow's breakers will be like a map of today
reach their crest spawn apples then die
in the empty silos of time
Echoes in the hollow granary return
as word shadows making spider web designs
with a few metallic screeches bats flap darkness
to sleep and dream with witch hazel eyes

One pearlescent fairy wing
is all that's left for a headstone
above a hole torn in space and time
Our crowded black wax words burn in sky burials
dark matter melts into the atmosphere
Prayers quiver in the hourglass
chained to crude oil and abattoirs
the horned serpent salvos lightning
and voltaic hail from its hooked beak
The battle ensues, swallowing consciousness
at the feeding trough
with too-late messages from the dead minute hand
on the sanctuary door knocker
jawbone of a fear lord muttering static

Swirling around us presence
without proportion or trope
Horizonless power of the mystery keeps me silent
for the arc and fall of ten thousand things
Sun chariots gallop with gilded hooves
through my Earth-headed vision
sparking creative rhythms
across frontiers of imagination
Scintillating the indigo incense smoke
fragrant diaphanous voices of revelation
wedged between worlds, leathery thunderbird
plumes pinned under the floorboards
Flayed with a pentacle in dark prophecy
appearances of animals just like me
in the unconscious wounds of time
breaking history, present and future
into digestible accounts of madness
The creation story's sickle moon
leaps back into the shattered mirror
My ink bearing hand moves through the omens
building power behind the throne
Writing sighs of falling leaves into the clock
Eclipsing the sun dial with the sweep
of my hand in the welkin
The runic bell tower surges with chimeric beings
valkyrie, jinn, geomancers and seers
Pendulums draft longing into my platelets
synchronizing dissident numerals
in my watchtower's tocsin metabolism
I find myself garbed in animal prints
and dappled gray river shadows
The dust rises from the approaching
Earth prophets in their ceremonial procession
They come to greet me
chanting through conifers, monkey-flowers
and shimmering turquoise dragonflies
Swallows form into a nomadic tent

For their arrival I place an altar inside
the artist's blank canvas
a tithe of lightning bolts
cornmeal and floral honey
A red human head effigy pot
of cactus flower nectars
Intoxicating beauties
to lure the holy stories back
I pluck the image lyre to merge
with the astromancer's unseen presences
Set the candelabra on fire
with colors of arroyo, gulch and sward

We all sit in council, coyote holds sway
with every hunting creature, wild plant and sage spirit
My totems wait outside by the Joshua tree
I can hear the yucca moth egg hatching
as far away as the coral seabed
swimming closer to listen to its destiny
Always the coyote - I think
with my hindquarters kicking
doctrine into metaphor
My white spirit horse fetish tethered inside
hemp twine taut as the bird tent guylines
I carry the frost of experience on pine bark
a rattlesnake calmly restrained
for one hundred years

We pitched camp here so wise
thoughts can slowly sink in to re-envision
heal the ghost Earth long gone
We exorcise the breed of humans
that destroy our sacred home
In this bivouac I can see myself clearly in the distance
wearing a blue cowl and white nimbus mask
I dream into the governing bodies of the universe
Lost and found eyes move like jellyfish diaspora

in vertigo of consciousness
sighing through my feeling tides
Invisible electric adrift in waterless water
Exiles storm-scattered over a deadening world
marooned far from our true nature

To you my body looks like a sharp angular door
Jaguar teeth in caked dried mud
or shadows of desert sand turning animalistic
somatic - serpentine in its cunning movement
Beyond it, a second door opens without warning
appears as a precipitous entrance to the underworld
Longhair curtains framing a pointed ear hollow
a gnarled corridor to a hissing old world story
written on lightning sheets in the darkness

A gatekeeper poised in the guise of the dead
hails you forward with his appraising eyes
When you become lost in the exodus
of all familiar things in his gaze
with palpable tenebrous whispers
he will open the hollow bone fence
with his velvet sheathed antlers
Your spirit will travel past his frame
of oily black beetle shells
green feathers fluttering around pale yellow eyes
Inside his fairy ring you can see life
on the other side, cats rising from the dead
verdigris skinned creatures staring obtrusively
others dancing wild in convoluted circles

Fear and fear not as he stirs
the clay vessel of salted fire
fresh bones and red wind
to keep at bay the growing shadows outside
Shard of an emissary's omniscient voice
splitting from the cavernous quartz

passes rumbling through his prescient body
Here you'll leave behind your culture and personality
your shrewd ivy strangling to reach its apex of smoke

Now find your way through
the four milled corners of the earth
carrying woven hemp bridges
from Fern Island to Moss Island
Cross the eternal bottomless swamp
growing frogs and lady's slipper
Earth Mother has laid before you
a piney headland
with a sacred vessel veiled in fog
Shove this swale nimble boat away
from the copper needled floor
Move over the moonlit marsh
swollen with spring flood waters
Your paddles make the only sound
in these shallows of quiet stillness
Take heed do not disturb the spears
of aberrated minds underwater

When you reach Crow Island
hidden in rippling rings
pick up the lady carrying a lute
with her small encampment of elven-owls
Cut left through the drifting grass
cattails and reed tips
Follow the smell of amniotic brine
musk and decomposition of apologue
You will see a chamber full
of violet moons in a velvet sky
Things will be said there
that have never been said before
clearing passageways
through the primordial soul
See the breath of her children

floating on stones
singing in the forest of mandolins
reading books inside mushrooms
on the mystery of humankind
star-spore windows perpetually open
to the giants with sheen of crow in their eyes

ANOTHER BREAKING OF BREAD INVITATION

Invisible outlaws and fugitives predicting our future
reemerge as ghost shamans
searching for the primal sun-lit core
of each letter made from the failing tongues
of sons and daughters of the earth
The crepuscular rays can change
any hand-sized geode
into a vast revered forest
The coral reef light shafts that can mutate
a sand grain on a deserted beach
into a verdant isle for lost mariners

Ancient *word* animals still roam
dispersed among the unknown
extinct species of Homo longi
from the land of the Black Dragon River
They still use their phonetic morphing
pictograph echolocation
as a tracking sense-ability
to see in the dark

It is by this method
cave crickets with volcanic glass-eyes
sow fractals of light
into the haunted unconscious troglodytes

By these same means barn owls drop
peace lily seedpods
into the abyss of the infernal devil's maw

By these common virtues forgotten
harmonic clay *words*
mold the beauty of the natural world
within the nothing so you will know

I am not a ghost I am not a ghost

But wither, sweat and dream of dark faces
Green knees, snow knives, erasers of time
herds and clan
As the forbearers traditional tools
are resurrected - their language alters my identity
in the Book of Changes

Before I start something new
in its pages of wind and water
I submit to the rite of cosmic cleromancy
and lose ten wings on the World Tree branches

I bleed magma and ash in seismic waves
From my freshly cooled lava I grow
dragon glass medicine from sacrificial fault lines
So now we look through ourselves
to see boreal bears painting the aurora
brushing lichen and moss in the foreground
daubing food and shelter in reach
of reindeer and caterpillar communiqués

My inner space words erase themselves
in a painting created by another monkish-self
and reappear in convergent evolution
nearer higher ground
They seek themselves in anonymity among the many
and in the many within anonymity

In the book without pages they catalyze the Qi
from square aspect ratio
to refashion disparate molecules
into a bristle of synergistic energy
rustling through husked corn
and murmuring through swamp orchid lady's slipper
we hear green soliloquies of healing silence

in the oosphere and fallow field
Jack-in-the-pulpit preaches of lore and vision
eroding together with our ancient tribes
into the river delta
All is not washed away from the stone ledges
but lives in the gathering word
tremulous as an apple blossom
fertilized deep in the womb
of a white grotto mare
- galloping off the cliff top
brays in mid-flight accountings
of the interpenetration of seven realities

My doppelganger spirit-painter
symbiotically sparks her light skin pigments
to change color in mid-flight
flickering an upward brush stroke
with a ferment of ambrosial fire
The burning drips of glassy nectar and resin
illuminate how we're tethered
to writhing tensile ropes
of philosophic dust and rote prayer

In their dark heights cosmopolitan bees
drone through the underbelly of thundercloud
Their burgeoning herbal poems
vibrate in consonance curl and bud
converting intimate honey
into beeswax beneath flame
dancing irreverently light
backwards to shadow
beyond reach of pulpits and lecterns
hours unravel in a trance
of pantheistic eternities…

Can you feel the fluid heat of this embryonic script
gestating a floral mythos in its light amber sac

uttering its oracles in leafy soft syllables
Can you hear tributes and contracts of power
spelled out in bear paw glyphs in the mineral cavern
Translucent white wolf tracking
the healing herbs beneath the scree
deciphering the ministries of destiny
names of holy beings in towering cumulus congesti
Oaths and star signs pressed into clay tokens
rest in the dusty hall of the ancestral hermitage
Outside the courtyard is filled
with deities yarning, splicing new myths
expanding consciousness within and without
beyond their messenger's scriptorium
seven times seven revelations
from seven divine dimensions

We learned from their visionary accounts
that our seventh child will be a werewolf
with invigorating powers
he will wander with his storytelling
in all directions weaving lyrical travelogues
of mythopoeia, will give wind to black flying
medicine horses pulling
seven sacred wheels of energy
into the soul's attractor particles
Prehistoric sable wolves
anointed in seven Siberian fir oils
will sing quickening emanations
through veiled perceptions
I was pierced
to the crossbones at the waxing crescent
by these golden acupuncture needles for seven hours
I was made to understand the deeper celestial rhythms
of the seven sleepers vibrating in the body's blood
I saw the colossal flying turtle
circling our unwritten records
in the disordered subatomic religion

There was never a battle of the holy birds
We fabricated this parable
to acquit ourselves of responsibility
for the tragedy of our darkness
Prevail poem! among the devourers and deceivers
incoherent satiety of hollow masses

May the last words of their thoughts
vanish without sound
Bees will not travel to their fruit or iron core
or sulfur smoke or stagnant water
The cave is too deep for their fearful reach
They will not crystallize soul
or be parasitical to the souls of others

Our ant couriers of the dead
heave the purifying daily bread up
For scouring the world of false tongues
I scatter its sustenance
among the broken colonnades of ancient council
Coyote daemon tracks the movement in my eyes
watching barbed kings and cursed queens
running through our bloodline
preying on the sacred weave of life
breaking the whistle in the wind
with murky secular distraction
An aerial spirit with feathered tongue
sends for another weaver bird
whose song rings through the earthstar
as a multiplied and undivided
invitation to break bread

THE FOUNT, THE ROOT AND THE RITE

I appear in many shapes and forms
In pattern, contour or guise I am the source
The fount the root, child of nebula and nova
I am the master of your animal body's drive
to the capricious moon's madness
From the office of the dead
I convulse cloud breath into portents
All will be blessed
crossing the boundary of my haunted mirrors
with their habituated generic half-life
I hold the mirror up to the self-deceiver
who deflects, averts, covers up
shifting vulnerability and blame
to scapegoats and sacrificial lambs

I know the ninety-six Sanskrit words for love
For love I have watched the jeweled facets
of death angels in rhythmic transfiguration

My home is a nascent narrative like yours
filled with tree moths, pigeonholes
and withering flowers, in my mind you will find
the beginning and end of the serpent-mind
coiling through calcified mirages
with syllables of scythes and arrowheads
I am the pause between breaths
in the primeval alphabet garden
and the loneliness that can't be held
with dead anecdotes or restless organisms
I am the dream without sleep
before the earth turned blue

My unhinged door is a storm cloud
of your pent-up anger battering the air

your outworn ghost my recent unfamiliar
Door handle a rainbow refraction
of your reflections and a few stray birds
who sigh at life's folly
The chair inside is made
from a tornado and a movie
moving further and further away
to see your distance
in the unfolding mystery
I am inside you when you turn
your thoughts my way
when you sense the other within
When you leave the selfdom
present yourself to the shadow
of the grizzled warden on the way out
Really a cunning impersonator of yourself
he carries the keys you gave him
on the way in
Some days I idle about
as a disruptive revisionist
on the ground of your being
A barnacle attached to a rusted hull
A parable banished to exile
sneaking secret messages into your pilothouse
I am your abandoned spirit port
lost on the far side of a pelagic map
Sunken in a seabed of sighs
a double helix propeller of the DNA
mindlessly whirling strange feeling tides
ciphers in an epic poem
with visions that purify perception

My sky spouse laces the air
with compressed shadow minutes
She outdoes herself
with spacious cosmic thought
No one gives her the eyes of dead stars

when I'm around
I'm seen
as her dreaming blue coyote
yipping my comical trickster fervor
for medicinal scraps, and divine creative powers
antitoxins for these dying times
Sometimes the undigested words you serve me
reside in the burning nucleus of your body
Pull them through your windowpane
watch ice melting in silence downwind
Keep your eye on impelling relationships
that require thoughtful attention
Everything else is the empty gestures
of dull existence filling blank corners
until everything is demystified with artificial facts
in a flat line until the end
The age of darkness

Exhaustive compromise
entering worldly ambition
increases emanations of dark matter
Self-obstructive pressure
nudges the need for deep change
with apprehensive self-arbitration
Ongoing serrated interpretation
compels automatous self-volitive maneuvers
into interstellar equilibrium

With your phantom hands and bone flutes
direct your complex emotive identity matrix
toward meteor fragments blending into the horizon

Instinctive parts of you will approach
know and sense all things disappear
but bloom elsewhere when we give
sacred attention to the dormant berry
of the heart - reddening to drop ripeness

into the extinct totemic and present moment
Fall again as dry leaf past live oak window
of the verdant queen's soul
who watches over all
who watches over all
Unaware you return her gaze
as she beckons your disappearing Qi
back into her bird-like source
so you might see your arrested light
sleeping on amnesia's immortal pillow
It is your vital force that amplifies to combust
and contracts to refashion
the tailor-made raiment
for your death song submission
Empty your secular ideation
into its law of nature
to return from the dead
in the clicking of a trillion beach pebbles
no one can separate us
flowerless brambles
brainwashing diversions
fissures in the pulse of reality
If you remain a sage stillborn
I will pass into the midwife
who fosters the wisdom
I am the fingerprint
on the misshapen
skeleton key to the master
before the earth was born
You - the modern detective
who searches for my love story
in the cloud breath
the ideograms of Tao light
in the fuchsia streams of pollen
Some try to swim the umbilical back
to untie their knot underwater
unravel the latitudes of mind

between pages of ornamented history
an obscured lost language of the earth
colonized by alienating polarities
reduced to miming what once was
the last bird sounds eradicated
by the deforestation of our minds
The Serengeti hunting for its animal feeling
in the last acre of silence
Star-father schisms, devouring
entitled patriarchs plotting
on the dark side of the moon
All the evening skies
that were once your own
shadow across the battery of breath

Moving her arms around all who never loved her
Earth shakes gravely the drowned
vermilion scrap heap of captains
capsized in the blood
I wait like a hermit with snake eyes
coiled to strike omega dissolution in its nucleus
I wait like a man with eagle feathers for arms
hungering to open your dormant heart's passageway
from the "I" into the "we" into all manner of beings

One wild holy word
carved from the ancient calendar wheel
can excite the tenderest thinnest branch
into an eagle-headed winged genie
As purifier and pollinator
the seraph she-devil staggers
the frozen light of cities
built upon the ash of villages
Aged and leaking child light
slips over the escarpment

There was a time and space

between the two world trees
when you knew birds sang rain
and muddy ponies put spells on apples
with creation-sounds
That all things live inside the other
That the sheen of an evergreen
might be enough to teach you
for the rest of your life

This story is too old for most of you
Do you know that it could furnish you
with a burning flower for a quick life
or a long oak belly weighed down in the clay
I'll tell you things you'll soon forget
But return again if you are ever kind to my kind
and we will begin again in the slight tear
between the beautiful harvest and virgin awareness

I see your holy human print fading in the mud
with a mended life growing beside it
I am the mask you want to remove
and I am behind it
The shadow of your world
when you stop growing
I wear the crop circles as tattoos
under a robe of stars
spread in every direction
I am the metamorphic strata
inciting your indigenous tongue
to unfold your soul-honed vision
in a sonorous healer's cry
I am the last scent of summer croon
released from the glowing azure
where butterfly wing tips
meet in the air above their bodies
I am the ink scrawl of dire words
tracking the spirit of the last puma

scrambling over the bodies
with flint-knife minds
I am the ancient grinding of corn
returned to the heraldic bones of swans
and the unmoored conch
blown by the sea-monk
trumpeting the dawn of a new world
I am the stepping-stone let loose
falling to learn the depths of ascent
The moonlit ink stroke divining
the ravaged glyphs of orphaned words
Words that know their stems were ripped
from the hardened Earth crust

I am the faded handprint
still working its way through
long gone valleys red with your blood
wrinkling maps of time in the before time
when the many rivers were woven
to make your forest dress
worn by the old mountain bones, saints of death
I am the magpie hand seeking
the Indian yellow glow in your ash mound
My silhouette sharpens your smoldering horizon
churning life stories into sirocco winds
If I am the rainbow bee
in your small flowered heart-throne
may your consciousness ferry its nectar
through the processing terminus
clear the long custom lines
and detention areas between us
I see the black dot under your question mark
weary in its reflection of moving forward
Siege of the unconscious and counterfeit powers
I am the prism of your singular thought
All things that you ever forgot
The outside mirroring inner experience

the inside mirroring outer
May we meet on the shores here
and know each other by all our eyes have seen
Blessed by the feathers of speech
may we recognize this passage in time
to catch each other in the darkness
by our reaching light

My silky spider thoughts climb
the reed-spire to the sun
gathering wisdom of the shrinking dew
the spear bends back to ground
to hear the earth's decree in elliptical orbits
Hackled orb-weavers can rearrange your plans
Rearrange your insides until you have many eyes
Can walk sideways with nimble grace
Can fly light-filled thread in poetic communion
Can resurrect presences in the moon's womb
Four sheep in the belly of a green field
Green field in the belly of the herd
Four crows in the head of an oak
waiting for the mollusk moon
to draw out the raven tribes
from high desert plateau

Raven flies the gossamer azurite prayer
mediates the trade routes to the mesa face
Heavy gloss-black plumage lifts their village song
in aerobatic leaps of ecstatic ceremonial dance
Sacred whistles trill lonely, mystical
returning petrified mountain shadows back to sky
I am watched from the foothills
by the ancient painted corn people
I am the soft turtle sky and colliding clouds
The mood of winter fire
among masked cliff dwellers
under the Corvus constellation

I hear bull roarers
amplifying the sky's syntax
with the soul echo of each little thing
With skilled birdsong
and traces of high myth
With their dogs barking
for the world to be whole
They rattle their shaman pebbles
into the star shined puddle
Hurl smoke rings and bird shine
through the watch tower of your body
Pull you through vast halls of the crowded mind
through clay maps of invisible borderlands
With medicine chant they lure you
into the epiphanic drowning spell
Let go - feel your old self
fall through the muddy mirror door
always open before you knock
Tapping on you before you open
They ferry your soul
through the growth rings
in the two World Trees
Welcoming land spirits press in
They know the most
remote places can be loved
I am Lunar and Solar chasing each other
in desperate love
the hummingbird feeding
on the sugar of their thoughts
When sun leaves, the moon turns in reflection
urges sacrifice for the fertility of the land
moonlight for covens and sunray for hives
Grief offerings for dead friends and animal deities
sleepless ghost brothers and sisters

Dark gods and goddesses of the unconscious
have you pierced the veil of sated delusions

devouring the holy heart
scattering tribes and cosmologies
What news is there of community
brothers and sisters
Let us make our way
through these rites of passage
to the root and fount of life

PHANTOM HANDS

The inscription below was written by a blind druid
The words spiral around an adder stone
If you were to look through its flint eyelet
you would see the end of this world
and the beginning of the other

My hands grow larger as I get older
mountainous sentries of withered afflictions
Broken bones, scar clenched maps
of pulsing purple light, seawater pools
absorbing comet dust clouds
Axe aching animal hands articulating the landscape
Curled bear-hair knuckled claws
bulge past their membranes
for the uppercut - foxgloves
The infant is still in these paws
little fists of rainstorms and fire pits
Ungloved mountain flower Qi coursing through
far-reaching inner stream, ritual hand
dorsal mitt, cutting incandescent dance smoke

If you extend your giving-hand
into the synapses of interwoven life
use fingers of dawn magenta
to write well into the earth
A new cobalt day will move through handcuffs
Remote transparent sky hands
will place cupped bird whistle filament
and hummingbirds giddy on sugar water
on the saguaro hands sticking out of the foothills
Can you tell me why one hand holds the outside
of another hand as a makeshift refuge
from the arthritic bones of the postmodern world

There's an empty shell inside my hand
that comes out for burials
inside the isolated ellipsis
When one forgets who is who
what is what in the venous network
my hands debone themselves
to get inside dark tight spaces
I see their whorled prints grappling
to relieve the enshrined ancestors
trapped behind our stoic walls

With empathic braille hands we sense
their unreadable cells in arcing leaps of blood
we feel their carbon-twinned images
but we cannot see their ascension
trailing ribbons of shadow
or hear our own resigned
uninhabited voices in the simulacra
My primal hand emerges
from the gray flint aperture
seeking warmth from the empty clear sky
with primitive excitement it crawls up pine roots
filled with moonlight and frost - phalanges
encounter wolf spiders baring fangs
like projectile points
hand jumps away detaching from body
and rises to become thunderclouds
at the end of an ice age
Will my woolly hand return
to dig through the decayed vegetation
dripping dissolved peat tannins
from my coarse long broken nails
scraping bog bodies
eating lumps of butter
from deerskin bladders
Will cold wet paleo-hands return floating
from their tombs like Saturn ice moons

Will they recall the quickened passions
enclosed in arched palms soft psalms
The right palm holds a fox skull
filled with thrush song and marsh thistle
The left holds chestnut horsehair
riding the rolling grass heights
verdant abode of the praying mantis
above the blustery sea
The mare's undulating body expanse
covers the wounds of grappling hooks
and rusted chains, the drowned
underwater dreams of perennial resurrection
Inside the vision tunnels lacuna
phantom hands grip and shake
their collective spirits together
One hand holds a large eye
filled with stories from Andromeda
another holds lightning in a terrarium
with a thermonuclear map legend
beyond the margins
Seen and unseen the cartographic symbols
sink deeper into wrinkles in time
to reemerge wizened by the unknowable mystery
They come back to extol the wisdom of hands
immersed in artistry, one hand dreams around
the knapped stone's axial tilt
fingers rotating around me
while the other hand sleeps in its flesh

Hands of silence on the impermeable cave wall
I extend my prayer hand to touch
your ocher palm lines holding memory
imprints of a disintegrated atlatl
As for amulet hands I wear my own
For these incongruous events on Earth
I orbit my hands to see the back side
the dark side organism mutating in polytheistic

demonology scrimmages with angelology
trophies awarded in ontology and epistemology
Shamanistic talismanic palm light slowly filters
through my webbed phalanges
Dream catchers of alien life forms
in longhand divinization transmissions

One cannot sate the wind of scarecrows
in their handicraft and counterfeit vocabulary
ignorant hands flapping with stormy appendages
imploding isolated test-tube baby social structures

The world is not enough anymore

I stick my unyielding hands to the universe
and they stay there
Even after death
handless
my phantom hands talk to me
through the poem yet to be written
around this hole
I have no choice
but to revere the palmists
and these handlers
in their ancestral halls
They dictate life
with such absurd authority
Their shadows pilot the face of this stone-page
to the last word spiraling around the hole
In the future of this book
will you see the imperceptible traces
of the one hand
holding a creature from the otherworld
while the other holds a cup of wrinkled stars
high above the pedantic deductive logic circuits
And will you know my transfigured nature body
has hands that are untraceable travelers

Subatomic buddhas playing with elliptical electrons
Jesuses of thorns making violet fields
of consciousness grow new azimuths
from old lifelines
The world was created with a hole
and through it two phantom hands are proffered
One offers protection on the pilgrims' road
The other offers capital assets
Choose before it's too late

THE ARK

A descended mariner from the she-god's womb
I am five hundred years old and still
piloting the deep end of her passing thought
before the first word was spoken by a chthonic serpent
through ancient religions and animal-headed visions
I'm directed to perform the sacred story dance
keeping step with space-time
floating movements to keep
the creatures stimulated to the bone
two by two, bipeds too
keeping them lively below deck
ready for deluge and regeneration
I chant sea shanties in call and response
striking gongs and whirling dervishes
enchanting spells swell
in vociferous clamoring
rip currents foam, crest and break
the hardened currents beneath the deep
black and blue skin of cities
glazed by the fury of locusts
Babel's unholy din
Who are we after all
in our myopic tower
seeking the rainbow hewn
into the crushed mirror expanse
We few survivors of the mass dimming perception
friends of the unfallen Watchers in the ark
Inside this microcosmic model of the universe
there's a hieroglyph of a hundred doves rising
sixty cubits from the interior's fresco
Wing of the heavens
vibrate in my breath
announcing secrets of immortality
in the fluttering smell of hull-less gopher wood

an alluvion torrent of hourglass sand
The depth of this moment
travels the ultramarine spirit cord
to the height of my collarbone
White spray of flying fish and blue-lipped sea krait
animates my attention to an amplified instant
a silent illumination in the koan's umbilicus
following the pulse of a streaming long haiku
inspiriting my lifeboat to glide over the watery earth
above the jagged coral reef
elevated with my salty naval salutations
writhing with electric eels
Land Ho! Ahoy! intertidal insects whoop
through their cerulean gills
Their silver tails trail shimmering rhythms
of silver veins over seven stepping-stones
in the surf seven days of the week
for the seven wonders of the world
primeval angels spread out seven
musical notes on thin sheets of water
They disperse through stellar-fields
and glistening lichens on fossil limestone
They inhabit my too few words
with just the right amount of shooting stars
to singe my locus of perception
and palpitate what I think
into a hoary group of idiosyncratic vowels
adding flames to my elocution
Word photon fuel for the speed of rainbows
envelopes my peculiar constitution as an adherent
who bonds ions to the electrically charged zero
In this nowhere space-time of death symbol phobia
I am able to write magically onward
through hunting coyotes and ghost deer ceremonies
Their shadows dance like clear running water
cascading over crushed stone
My filtering awareness in the porthole gathers

whirlpools of inconsistencies and symmetry
mending words that sink into the pressed
ink of this poem still lashed
to fixed reality's monotone
post-modernists' subconscious fog
Below decks the ark is unsuitable
for an underworld voyage
I'm a ghost face in a movie you're still watching
vanishing meanings aberration of light in a vacuum
Searching for a parable in a loop of shortsighted stories
weary of shrouded wrecks, underwater mastheads
outcrop of dark earth's wounded flesh
I keep manna from heaven in a pot
I keep it close to me inside a gold-plated cube
too small for the naked eye to view
It keeps us free of scurvy, seasickness and superstition
It quickens our seventh sense in the portal
when we start losing direction
in the cauldron of unknown planes of existence
Still far off the masked dawn's center axis
flutters like a key in a hole in a cloud
an angel wing sweetened and charred
by my excited feelings
I will change the way of passing elliptical days!
In this time and in between times
when there's no meaning
between these lines in the now now now
remain present as the visceral beauty of our nature
grows so near -
an olive branch grows from ancestral roots
clutching the heavens around my hurricane lantern
My ark-helm fills with vegetative symbols
and reverberating inflections
of the fiery sacred *word* coiling between these lines
Solar-light rays strike the ship's wooden wheel
time dilates and contracts in the spinal column
The Watchers surge and sing invisible mystical names

through grove, mountain and spring
I hear my aboriginal name unfurl
from Mesopotamia's Ur
A host of phenomena propagates curves
and bends, but you see only what you want
Particles of my many selves in relationship to you
implode in inelastic collision
Colossal towers of babble crash
into the sea of our complexity
canon doctrine dogma paradigm propaganda
frozen fire and sea monsters of our time
If the pressure and stress of a black hole
causes the core to collapse into supernova
why not seek the gravity of life
Let our terrestrial bodies fall
to the center of the earth
Land Ho! See there, the orange butterfly
grooms its stallion legs in the azure air
oracular scrolls flutter above crow's nest, that's a sign!
I'll unroll one and use it as a sail on the center axis!
I smell the dust rising off the land in heat waves
Caravans of camels, sheep skin yurts, nomadic souls
Bone fragments of mermaids, giants and Ganesh
dancing off grid, silent, in the undulating threshold
Gilgamesh, Ogre and the shade of Van Gogh!
I feel my beryl hand rising to shake hands
with the devil's tail, the Griffin's paw
will stroke the lion's mane
to calm the central nerve running
from planet to exoplanet
I cast my thought experiments
into the thorax of a sphinx
into trough and swell
of this rolling sapphire scrawl
skyward and plunge riddling
side to side shore to shore
my mythopoeic croon

for the unheard, untaught, unlearned
unspoken worlds of sonorous sounding
Watchers from the sediment of the ark
spread out between these pages
Set sail again on an ancient sacred poem
Cast light upon the swelling tide of darkness

THE UNWRITTEN CONTRACT

Only when it is snowing hard
and everything is thickly covered
And most people are inside and animals sheltered
Tracks enveloped and the horizon veiled
Whipping wind bites with searing needles
long before black frostbite of cheeks and chin
fingers numb toes burn and sting
Everything wet with the sound of my boots
Pushing pushing and dragging dragging
Carving shin deep in the alabaster
in the bleach frosted silver pearl
With my shepherd dog up ahead
like graphite on canvas
tracing the way home
Both of us steam-breathing overheating
And concealed ice slip slip and recover
and the sweat and silence
of it all making itself be known
in thousands of muffled but sure ways
The heaving and cracking of the marsh
and crackle of sparking glass-encased branches
Heavy thump of clumps dropping off
A few dizzying crows vanish
in distant light-gray smoke
It is like how life is meant to be
laden boot lightening from time to time
And I would think coffee and a shower
but not now, not now, maybe
And maybe I could keep going
for one more corner one more tree
Or the deer that would crack me in two
in the sheer joy of presence
Then that would be all
And I would go home and tell no one

And there would be no one to understand
And the thing, this thing, this whole thing
would live inside me like a cloven hoof rune
A living wet thing beneath
the transparency of my hoary thoughts
A tempest of cold gray trees
talking to me in high occult
Birds I could not see
not in this weather inside myself
But I can hear them
in the close familiar distance
calling me to believe
the earth is more than I ever imagined
And winter would stay with me
by the fire idle talk
A thin black bough of it taps
the hoar-glass pane, like fingernails clicking
the frozen zero of mercury to rise
it wavers in the wind, tip-taps
breaks the icicles it woodenly bends in
Colludes with my river of consciousness
not yet iced over
It waits for me tomorrow
my shepherd my walk
Already waits waits for me from tomorrow
Tomorrow already it says
but I wait for it
while it waits for me
with an unwritten contract I am bound to
and a few more I am sure of it
The ache in my waiting
the layered weight of my trudging
Freeze of my crystallized finger bones
Throes of this love that tires me
gives more comfort than all in-between

THE LAST HEALER'S MYTH

At the end times…
Earth was void and without form
Light could not comprehend the sphere's darkness
for the celestial body was stricken
defleshed shrieking chaos
bones extracted and blood drained
in a tower of numbed silence
Dark overseers - greed and vanity
reigned with their black arts
consuming the world's lost souls
their relationship with the deep
- Earth was not

Flood and fire lay waste
All was dissolution
but for a burnt brown March hare
madly darting through the heart's darkest interior
A morphing rustic thatched cottage of cracked walls
broken furniture regrowing in thick damp air
rubble heaving with the dusty Child of Prague
decapitated, abandoned clay effigy still waiting
for the pious ghost relations to return and mend
the shattered white dish on the moss table -
a final offering for hungry shadows and mold spore
Sanctus Patricius still not fed, dons the green ivy
and snakes around the crumbling corner stone
slowly turning into a berry
Just past ripe the blood red haw
drops for famished kin
long gone in turf smoke
Generations devoured in priestly drama
behind tear-streaked windows
Mad phantom-hare is hemmed in
braced in a shivering crouch

When I knock at the russet door
her wild bead eyes abandon her
quickening fires dancing in their black hearths
With a twitch of her tattered curtain ear
she sprints out through the smeared mirror
wild rearing daemon prophetess
hind feet beat a galloping leap
over garden Pan's moss-haired head
rousing cracked stone lips of Aramaic poetry
and releasing coyote psalms
from trapped musky air pockets
wedged between clouds
The soft lilting onomatopoeia of nature
frees the ancient hares imprisoned form

The light's all-seeing eye sees the all-in-all
The smoking birth cord and the last healer's breath
under the galactic world tree
The midwife wields the chthonic scythe
like a quarter moon crucible
through the black widow's veil
rocks and croons with its rising and falling
filaments - soft whispering surgical rhythms
The scribal goddess grunts and howls
memories and dreams of the creation-poem
facedown sweating in the wet matted grass
mutations of death in molecular evolution
crack open your earth animal skin
engraved with ancient myths
She shakes the turtle shell - shrill - rattle
into this moonless dead of night
through the haunted timbre
of treeless wolves
and twisting bear shadows
to the outer rim of your understanding -
dewdrops reflecting all other dewdrops
in dawn's translucent gossamer

Glittering with elemental insights
she reanimates the world
from the mausoleum's cobwebbed delusions
a thousand identities dispersing
quivering spirit particles
through the primordial birth canal

To fit the needs of impossible times
your animal body is crooned over
in mnemonic intoning
A light-bearer's allegorical story
of dismemberment's metamorphosis,
seeds, the sacred mound in the center of the village
Your sandals fill with Taoist's essence and bee droning
sweetgrass and quartz sediment from alluvial plains
The transmigration of your spectral double
looks for ways to track the masked dawn
to regrow denatured minds
to enter the bewitched dark shadows of their being
- moving through arterial corridors
with repeated focus repeating repeating
widdershins invocations
reversing the overlord dictates
to unmask their misspellings spinning
Earth backwards with afflicted hour hands
on the cryptic blackboard of no man's land
A flashback recalls
reliving each wounded letter
of each consecrated song word
bearing love's authority lightly
into covenantal destiny
Neurotransmitters and respiring rhythms
of written symbols fine-tuned to the medicinal arts
cure the divide between decay and eternity

In the burnt-out tundra of the starfields
I keep a healer's curved blade

safe in my body with protection spells
I keep drumbeats and deific idioms
of the toothed whale flickering on the marquee
for wayward attention spans
I keep the swallows' chiming locution
peeping from their mud huts
winged solaced tongues
scrying the sky map
in sinuous luna swirls
I keep deer words that utter snow
to the dead language listeners
I vibrate inside the Pleiadian Sisters' poems
blazing light trails
that pass out of existence
in deep fugues of sibilant amnesia
These words you walk upon these words
are mythopoeic taproots
cycling through the autonomous crossroads
fossilized articulation of the great
aeonian prayer wheel
In wind-driven hail
with your unformed wings
fly out of body
erase yourself and return like a bull-roarer
from the anesthetized falling sky
with your uncharted presence
and immaculate conceptions
of visionary images and sound receptors
hearing the strangely familiar - Earth-diving bells
Seraphic guitar strings
reaped from the other side
To reenact your sacred play
with the purring weightless alphabet of this tale
conscripting you and keeping you
on the lightning roads of your spirit body
Cultivate a new Earth story
for times of great hunger and of great power

Use the life-giving words
reoriented from parallel dimensions
words from your own future
bordering the fringes of temporal perception
Magnified mirrors from other constellations
fill your windowpane with emotions
to make you think on stranger things
to stir you out of your darkroom
and out of the darkening ranks
of the underworld's cold statecraft
married to the corporate board of directors
with the chairman's thundercloud mistress
flanking the last remaining coastline
Her gatekeepers and sentries howl
and haunt your dreams and bring you homeward
to serve the mysteries time after time
with catchments of lighthouse light
beneath the sands of eroding time
your inner sanctum
illuminating winter stories of sanctuary

In the beginning...
when the hare was on the moon
making immortality elixir for mortals
you could hear the pounding
of the pestle in her meteroite mortar
and see the light images of medicine herbs
emanating as a lunar halo
Perceptive humans still hear and see
these things at this present moment
It was a summoning time
for the dance of the corn maidens
to guide hummingbird song narratives
into numinous sounds proclaiming
revelations of wisdom's beauty
in the rose-colored dawn
It was a time for the listening

restless coyote trickster
full of magic and labyrinthine soliloquy
to shadow the emerging humans
as they were returning back
from their antipodal cycle
He deceived them into sacred ways of living
lest they had forgotten
what happened in their last end time
Now in what manner will you live
coyote asks, in sleep, wake and dream
for the light to recognize you
coming home unmasked
with a perceiving sentience
of a different kind
knowing how to dance
with powers of nature

CPSIA information can be obtained
at www.ICGtesting.com
Printed in the USA
BVHW051944040123
655552BV00019B/131

9 798986 780405